D0652094

# Transforming Love

# Transforming LOVE

### HOW FRIENDSHIP WITH JESUS CHANGES US

## AMY BOUCHER PYE

**Our Daily Bread**
Publishing.

*Transforming Love: How Friendship with Jesus Changes Us*
© 2023 by Amy Boucher Pye

All rights reserved.

Requests for permission to quote from this book should be directed to: Permissions Department, Our Daily Bread Publishing, PO Box 3566, Grand Rapids, MI 49501, or contact us by email at permissionsdept@odb.org.

Scripture quotations, unless otherwise indicated, are taken from the Holy Bible, New International Version®, NIV®. Copyright © 1973, 1978, 1984, 2011 by Biblica, Inc.™ Used by permission of Zondervan. All rights reserved worldwide. www.zondervan.com.
    Scripture quotations marked GNT are taken from the Good News Translation in Today's English Version—Second Edition. Copyright © 1992 by American Bible Society. Used by permission.
    Scripture quotations marked KJV are taken from the Authorized Version, or King James Version, of the Bible.
    Scripture quotations marked NRSV are taken from New Revised Standard Version Bible, copyright © 1989 National Council of the Churches of Christ in the United States of America. Used by permission. All rights reserved.

Interior design by Jessica Ess, Hillspring Books

ISBN: 978-1-64070-228-8

*Printed in the United States of America*
24 25 26 27 28 29 30 31 / 9 8 7 6 5 4 3 2

Two are better than one,
because they have a good return for their labor:
If either of them falls down,
one can help the other up.
But pity anyone who falls
and has no one to help them up.
Ecclesiastes 4:9–10

To amazing friends and family who enrich my life:
Beth—sister and friend; Kris—friends since three;
the FFF—through thick and thin; Tanya and Amy—
writers and poets; Ali, Anne, and Julie—prayer warriors;
Ali and Paul, Esther and Simon, Gill and Rob—friends
of my adopted land who've made me feel at home.

Friends always show their love.
What are relatives for if not to share trouble?
Proverbs 17:17 GNT

# CONTENTS

Introduction: Friends of Jesus . . . . . . . . . . . . . . . . . . . 9

## Part 1
### Being and Doing: The Luke 10 Story

Chapter 1: So Distracted . . . . . . . . . . . . . . . . . . . . .17

Chapter 2: Listening and Learning . . . . . . . . . . . . . . . .29

Chapter 3: Both . . . And. . . . . . . . . . . . . . . . . . . . . .39

## Part 2
### Grieving and Rejoicing: The John 11 Story

Chapter 4: Waiting for Jesus. . . . . . . . . . . . . . . . . . . .53

Chapter 5: Aftermath . . . . . . . . . . . . . . . . . . . . . .67

Chapter 6: At the Tomb . . . . . . . . . . . . . . . . . . . . .79

## Part 3
### Loving and Serving: The John 12 Story

Chapter 7: The Party. . . . . . . . . . . . . . . . . . . . . . .91

Chapter 8: Liquid Love . . . . . . . . . . . . . . . . . . . . 103


Final Words: The Encounter That Changes Us . . . . . . . . . 113

Acknowledgments . . . . . . . . . . . . . . . . . . . . . . . 115

Leader's Guide . . . . . . . . . . . . . . . . . . . . . . . . . 117

Notes . . . . . . . . . . . . . . . . . . . . . . . . . . . . . . 125

# Friends of Jesus

"Amy! Cross that out and don't write anything else!"

The command from the junior high school principal rings out, and I flush with shame. With haste I scribble out what I'd written: "Kris is weird." Avoiding the stares of my classmates, I step away from the wall designated for affirmations about other students.

After school, my stomach churning, I walk the few doors down to deliver a note to Kristen. *Oh, why,* I wonder, *did I write those words?* As I berate my thirteen-year-old self, I hope Kris will forgive me. Standing away from her as she reads through my note, I fidget. I hope that I haven't ruined things and that we can salvage our friendship.

After what seems a long time, she reaches to hug me and relief floods my insides. "I'm so sorry," I choke, trying to hold back the sobs. "I don't know why I wrote that. I . . . I'm sorry."

For a time our friendship stumbles along with uncertainty, but eventually I regain her trust. Her unreserved forgiveness touches me, and I know I'll never forget the grace she extends.

Fast-forward more than a few decades and Kristen and I share tears once more, but this time of gratitude. I look around the dining-room table in my parents' home in Minnesota and take in the sight of three generations of neighbors-turned-friends—Kris and her parents and daughter, me and my daughter and parents, and our next-door neighbors and their daughter and granddaughter. These friendships have been foundational in my life, providing a community that I rather took for granted when growing up. We're spread out now, from Colorado to London with several places in between, but when gathered together we give thanks for how God has shared his love between us, including the many years we ran between the houses on Victoria Street.

My friendship with Kristen holds a powerful place in my heart not only because we've been friends pretty much our whole lives—her family moved to our street when we were three and four years old—but because of how God has shaped me through her. She's spoken truth to me lovingly when I've needed to hear it and has showered me with encouragement and cheering. We've studied the Bible and prayed together and have simply had fun with each other. Through her friendship, God has helped me to become more like Jesus.

I wonder if you too can call to mind longtime friends who hold a special place in your heart or those people whom you connected with immediately. When we receive this gift of friendship, it's like the Spirit within us leaps in recognition of each other; something inside clicks, and we know that a bond has been formed. We are granted welcome in their soul, just as we welcome them into ours. This openness of spirit—this extravagant generosity when it comes to letting others in—comes from an openness to God. He floods our soul with his Spirit, and the Spirit flows onto those we meet.

When Jesus lived on the earth, he had close friends whom he loved and who cared for and loved him. His friends were not only his band of disciples but also a trio of siblings who lived in Bethany, a village less than two miles from Jerusalem. Mary, Martha, and Lazarus welcomed him into their home, and their abode became Jesus's place to rest and feel at home. Just as I ran over to Kristen's home, making my way behind the houses with the joyful thought of seeing her, so too do I imagine Martha opening the door to Jesus and receiving his welcoming smile. And I ponder how much affection Jesus showed them. In fact, John's gospel names these siblings specifically as those Jesus loved (11:5). After his mother, Martha and Mary are probably the most important women in Jesus's life.[1]

## Friendship with God

I find it awe-inspiring to think that the God of the universe came to Earth as a baby. And that Jesus desired companionship with others. He needed friends, which he found in the band of disciples whom he did life with, but also these siblings from Bethany who gave him a space to rest away from life in Jerusalem. And God still desires friends today.

Think about that—God made us to relate to him. God created people not because he had to but because he wanted to. Then and now, God desires that we would seek him out in love, sharing with him our desires, fears, and accomplishments. Even as he reveals himself to us through Jesus and the Spirit, so too does he long for us to show ourselves to him.[2]

But sometimes fear crowds out our feelings of friendship with God. We might think of God as a distant parent, one whose demands we cannot meet. Or a disappointed judge whom we fail. Or an unconcerned being who doesn't really care for us. Or a fickle friend who plays favorites, skipping over us again. But with any and all of these conscious and sometimes unconscious feelings, we can trust that our loving Friend will help us to uncover and overcome them.

Because as we deepen our friendship with Jesus, we become more fully ourselves. We receive affirmation from God, which sets us free from a desperate need to please others. We find we can focus on the projects and tasks we feel called to do, instead of those others might foist on us. We can share our love with others without being stingy, knowing that God will give us more and more love to share. And we can celebrate the wonderful accomplishments of those whom we might be tempted to envy, those who flourish in the areas we inhabit. As we reach out to them in friendship, we come to understand that God blessing them doesn't stop God from blessing us. Friendship with God blesses us in all of these ways and in many others too.

I wonder what you're thinking and feeling as you consider friendship with Jesus. What longings churn within you (such as for a close relationship with him, for affirmation and love, and so on)? How is your life different because you know Jesus? How might he deepen your love for him and change you all the more? You might want to pause and ponder these questions, perhaps going for a walk as you invite Jesus to come alongside you. I trust that he will reveal himself gently and graciously. And that as you read this book, he will accompany you as we explore the story of some of his favorite people. Even as now *we* are some of his favorite people—a mind-blowing and life-changing truth.

## Changed by Love

When I think back to that awkward teenager who wrote hurtful statements about her friend, I temper the pangs of shame with compassion for my young self who so wanted to be accepted by her peers. Who, at heart, wanted to love and be loved. And although I can find it difficult in the moment to see how God changes me—especially if I've just lost it with a beloved family member—when I look back over the decades I can see the transformation that has come through God's Spirit living within me. Through friendship with God, I know that I am loved and can therefore share his love with others.

And this is what friendship with Jesus brings about; when we receive his love and affirmation, we grow more into the people God has made us to be. That is, we become more truly ourselves. We find peace and contentment as we bring to him not only our joys and praise but our fears, disappointments, and anger. We become better friends with others, as Kris and I did over the years. As we become intimate with him, God changes us to become more like Jesus, from the inside out. Even as Mary and Martha did, as we'll see.

Jesus transforms the sisters and brother as they encounter him in the ordinary and extraordinary moments of their lives. We'll explore how he brings Martha to a true understanding of who he is as the Messiah and who she is as one who serves and loves him. How Jesus affirms Mary in her desire to learn and be with him while also drawing her out of her deepest moments of grief and disbelief. How he effects great change for Lazarus—namely bringing him back to life.

I pray God will spark even more desire within you to meet with him and receive his love—and to be changed moment by moment as you do so. I pray that as you grow in your friendship with him, your relationships with friends and family members will deepen and flourish. As you read, you might want to hold in your heart one or two special people, asking God to show you how you can bless them. You could also ask God to give you a friend whom you can affirm and show love.

My prayer too is that you would sense God's nearness while engaging with these gospel stories, and so I've included prayer prompts and prayers in each chapter to invite you to an ongoing conversation with him. You might wish to write down your thoughts and prayers in a journal as you journey through the material—doing so gives the added benefit of you having a document to read later as a reminder of what you learned and experienced.

You might try out the prayer practices in a group—if you're leading it, see the guide at the back for tips and suggestions. If not, you might want to listen to me leading some of the exercises on my website.[3] Or you may prefer to do them on your own. Know that whatever your approach, God is with you and will guide you.

As you engage with these practices and think about the siblings from Bethany, trust that God longs to meet with you. As you encounter him and his goodness, may he change you moment by moment through his tender, kind, and unfailing love.

*Loving Father, Brother Jesus, Comforting Spirit, thank you for welcoming me to be your friend. Thank you for being near to me—for never leaving me or rejecting me. Help me to be open to your Spirit, that I would welcome you to change me in any and every way you wish. Give me a sense of expectancy for the ways you will move in power, grace, and love. Amen.*

## PART 1

# Being and Doing

## The Luke 10 Story

The famous story of Martha serving and Mary listening helps us, regardless of our gender, age, or status, to explore how we root our identity and our actions in our relationship with God. The snapshot from this day in Bethany helps us to embrace some of the tensions we face when we pursue both action and contemplation in our life with God.

# CHAPTER 1

# So Distracted

"Hey Jen," I say. "Will you read through my Christmas newsletter before I send it off?"

I started writing a yearly missive to friends and family in Minnesota after moving to the nation's capital midway through university. Now, a couple of years later, I'm looking for feedback from my housemate, especially because she's also served at the same small nonprofit with me. But her response jolts me.

"This sounds more like a work report than a Christmas letter!" she says. "You haven't said *anything* that doesn't relate to the organization."

I reread the letter and realize that she's right. Her observation gently chips away at the protective wall I've erected around myself to keep hurt and fear at bay. With a sense of clarity, I realize I'm a twenty-something who defines herself solely by what she does and produces. Or to put it more bluntly: I realize that I don't have a life outside of my work.

Her words set me thinking, and in the months that follow, I explore why I've made everything about my work. I realize I'm masking my insecurities by staying busy. My recent breakup with my fiancé shakes up my friendships, and I know I need to move outside my comfort zone to build some new relationships. Although I feel awkward, I resolve to go to the singles' group at church. I dread those first moments after walking through the door, but know I must push through my resistance and fears. I trust that I'll come to understand myself more through my interactions with others.

Sharing a townhouse with three women affords me plenty of opportunities to engage with others firsthand. As I digest the truth that God loves me, I have to ask myself why I struggle to live with, and love, my roommates who are also God's beloved. For instance, why do I resist when my roommate asks me to separate the forks, knives, and spoons by type in the dishwasher? Or why do I get so annoyed with the stomping overhead when they arrive home? I often overlook my own faults, but I feel a whoosh of humility when one of them shares an eye-opening insight with me. She recounts how while we were in the middle of a disagreement, she stood in the shower for a good long time while praying for me. She was seeking God's help to see me as made in his image so that she could show me love and compassion. Exactly what I'm trying to do with her.

As I grapple with my lack of awareness about what it looks like to live with me, I start to realize that throwing myself into my work helps me avoid facing the messiness of life with others. Yet I know that I won't grow in maturity if I simply hide away with my various projects. I want to learn how to enjoy resting and simply being while not acting on the compulsion to move to the next thing on my to-do list.

In these interactions and through my growing intimacy with God, I'm learning that I don't have to work and achieve to prove my worth. I start to understand not only in my head but in my heart that I am lovable simply because God created and formed me. Because I'm God's child, I can rest and simply be.

## Seeking Balance

I share this glimpse from my life in my twenties, as we explore the story of Mary and Martha from Luke's gospel, because I love to work. Sometimes I wonder if, with my heritage of both my parents growing up on farms, I have a deep-seated impetus to work. My maternal great-grandmother moved from Germany to America when she was thirteen, settling into life in Iowa with her parents on a farm. Her children—my grandmother—also grew up on a farm, as did my mother. The women in my family were raised plucking chickens, planting and harvesting food from the garden, preserving vegetables to eat throughout the arctic winter, and milking the cows. In order to survive, they worked.

That industrious spirit continues today, and if you were to drop into my parents' home unannounced, you'd find it spotless and clutter-free. Their white kitchen floor would be pearly white. They'd invite you in and defrost a wonderful baked delight to enjoy.

As I consider my heritage and think back to my twenties, I ponder whether now I'm more balanced with work, family, and recreation. My answer is, "Yes, but . . ." Yes, I often strike more of a balance then I did decades ago but no, I don't have it all figured out. My love of creating, producing, shaping, and achieving hasn't dissipated—I still enjoy immersing myself in a project and getting it done. And I still often find myself overcommitted, wondering why yet again I find myself in the predicament of looming deadlines amid a too-tight schedule. These years later, I still need the story of how Jesus loves Martha and Mary as he calls Martha to a better way.

## Examining the Story

In this chapter we're focusing on Martha from the story in Luke and how she let her tasks overshadow the invitation to sit at Jesus's feet and learn from him. But for an overview, let's dig into the narrative bit by bit:

> As Jesus and his disciples were on their way, he came to a village where a woman named Martha opened her home to him. She had a sister called Mary, who sat at the Lord's feet listening to what he said. But Martha was distracted by all the preparations that had to be made. She came to him and asked, "Lord, don't you care that my sister has left me to do the work by myself? Tell her to help me!"
>
> "Martha, Martha," the Lord answered, "you are worried and upset about many things, but few things are needed—or indeed only one. Mary has chosen what is better, and it will not be taken away from her." (Luke 10:38–42)

First, notice where this story appears in Luke's gospel. It's sandwiched between two crucial sections, the account of the good Samaritan (Luke 10:25–37) and Jesus teaching his friends to pray in what we know as the Lord's Prayer (Luke 11:1–4). Perhaps with this ordering Luke shows us first how to love and serve our neighbor (the good Samaritan), then the importance of listening to Jesus over serving him (Mary and Martha), then how to be heard by Jesus (the Lord's Prayer).[1] While God wants us to love our neighbor, even as ourself, he also wants us to prize our relationship with him.

## The Village and the Siblings (v. 38)

As Jesus and his friends travel, they arrive at the home of Martha in Bethany. With this village less than two miles from Jerusalem on the southeastern slope of the Mount of Olives, it wouldn't be a long journey for them. For further context, it's about four miles from Jesus's birthplace in Bethlehem.

In Aramaic, the common language they spoke, Martha's name means "owner" or "master." She's the firstborn in what may be this family of means, and although she's a woman, Luke names her as the head of the household.[2] Even in this first verse of the story, the Bible goes against the culture of the day. In the ancient world, the eldest male would be seen as the homeowner. He would be the one to greet visitors. In contrast, women would have very little interaction with men outside of their family.[3] But God breaks through the accepted conventions and empowers women according to their gifts and his purposes.

Why might Luke name Martha as the key person? Some commentators wonder if Lazarus doesn't play that role because he's incapacitated by some kind of chronic illness.[4] Physical limitations that prevent him from traveling would fit the pattern of Jesus visiting the home of the siblings in Bethany instead of them going to meet him.

## Martha Reacts to Mary and Confronts Jesus (vv. 39–40)

Another countercultural feature of this story is how Mary sits at the feet of Jesus, learning from him (which we'll explore more in the next chapter). Martha, in contrast, doesn't think she has time to sit at the feet of Jesus. She serves the Lord, who has arrived unannounced—it's not like he texted ahead to say they were coming! When he and his friends appear, she kicks into high gear and bustles around the kitchen as she makes the preparations. At that time, many were a woman's tasks—grinding flour, baking bread, tending the garden, spinning wool, washing clothes, cooking the food.[5]

Notice, however, that those many jobs don't include serving the meal to the men in attendance. That task would fall to a male servant.[6] But Martha, in wanting to see to Jesus's needs, breaks this accepted practice.

We see her presenting herself to Jesus, standing before him. In the Greek, the original language of the New Testament, the verb for *stand* has a sense of suddenness to it. She stands authoritatively.[7] And she says to him, in effect, "Don't you care? My sister's left *me* to do all of the work! Tell her to get up and help me!"

What we witness so beautifully is the freedom Martha feels in presenting herself to Jesus in this way. She can reveal her frustration to him; she can be open and even a little cranky. I think in our rush to judge Martha we may overlook how wonderful it is that she can share her exasperation with Jesus. She's not silently stewing in the kitchen and then making passive-aggressive comments to Mary. Rather she lays it all out before her friend.

## Jesus Responds to Martha (vv. 41–42)

As we view Jesus's response, note how lovingly he sees what's really going on in Martha when he calls her by name. He understands that she's worried and upset, with many things goading her. She's not invisible nor taken for granted but so important to Jesus that he names her *twice*. In the Bible, a repeated word signifies a greater level of importance.

Jesus sees that Martha is worked up and anxious, and he doesn't want to leave her in this state; he calls her to a better way of living. He understands that she's distracted by many things, but he wants her to focus on the one thing that's needed. That is, he invites her to make the most important thing in her life the most important thing. Instead of fretting, she can sit at the feet of Jesus—learning from him, loving him, being with him.

Jesus doesn't negate Martha's desire to serve, but affirms that Mary's choice of focusing on him is better and won't be taken away from her. Mary soaks in his wisdom and enjoys being with him.

## Anxiety-Inducing Work

Because I like to achieve and complete projects, I can relate to Martha in this story. I can imagine getting anxious and resentful over Mary sitting at Jesus's feet doing seemingly nothing while I slave away in the kitchen. When we host guests, for example, all of a sudden I see every cobweb hanging from the ceiling, all the piles of paper and clutter, every crumb and piece of dirt on the floor. I can become a bit of a madwoman as I whip the house into shape while seeking to employ my husband and kids in the task.

Like Martha in this scenario, I'm distracted and frustrated. I can be thinking about Wi-Fi codes and wondering if our guidebooks to London are up to date while forgetting that Jesus is with me. I let the distractions of preparation take over as I seek to create a welcoming space while I often overlook the other inhabitants of our home. Including Jesus.

But Jesus welcomes me to release my cares to him. He told his disciples not to worry but instead to trust God: "Do not worry about your life, what you will eat; or about your body, what you will wear . . ." (Luke 12:22). He went on to say how much God cares for even the ravens, who have enough to eat without storerooms for grain (v. 24). And when he sees Martha so anxious and upset, he realizes just how much she's weighed down. The word Luke uses in the Greek suggests that Martha being troubled exceeds that of an individual worry; she's taken on the cares of the community.[8]

## Equating Our Work with Our Worth

In my daily life, I can slide into defining myself by my work. That is, I achieve my worth through the articles and books I write, the retreats I lead, the spiritual direction I give. The goal, I start to believe implicitly, is to make a difference through whatever project in which I'm currently engaged. But God doesn't love us for what we do. According to Jesus, "The work of God is this: to believe in the one he has sent" (John 6:29). Believing in God through Jesus, I can revel in the knowledge that I'm God's beloved, trusting that my identity rests on being his child and not on anything that I do or leave undone. God doesn't place all of that pressure on me, so equally I shouldn't take it on.

Why do we fuse together our identity with our work? The roots of this practice come from the curse of the fall (see Genesis 3). Before Adam and

Eve disobeyed God, he entrusted them to care for creation. Work at that time wasn't backbreaking but a sheer joy. But our first parents turned from God and ushered in sin and death, and in the process work became warped. Thorns and thistles started to crowd the healthy plants and the earth suffered droughts and floods. Tilling the land then entailed laboring over the dry and cracked soil and pulling out the choking weeds.

Today our work can be tinged with disappointment, exhaustion, and distress. We can too often align our identity with it and become distracted by it. We may feel hemmed in by the expectations we or others hold regarding work, whether those of our parents or mentors, society, or peers. One example is the assumptions people have over the work of parents of young children, whether you're a mother who works outside the home or one who doesn't, or a father caring for the children at home. Another example is how often, when we meet someone for the first time, our opening question is, "What do you do?"[9]

Our answers to these dilemmas can be shaped by the better way that Jesus calls Martha to—a relationship with him. Through our friendship with God, we experience the redemption of our work as we collaborate with God's Spirit in creative and life-enhancing ways. He spurs us on to believe, our main work. And he partners with us on exciting projects, enriching activities, and encouraging relationships that call forth the best and truest parts of ourselves. Working with God, we spend our time and energy in ways that spread his love and life in the world, making it a better place.

God also shows us how to lay down our projects at healthy intervals. We can form patterns of work and rest that reflect our human needs of sleep, exercise, play, and good nutrition. He feeds our emotional health too. As we relate to God daily, he pours into us the affirmation we long for—which we often seek through the approval of others.

## Time to Pray: Prayerful Reading

As we consider our relationship to God and our view of work, let's move to a time of engaging with this story prayerfully. I invite you to ask God through his Spirit to speak to you as you read the passage from the Bible four times, each time with a different emphasis. The steps of prayerful reading are reading, reflecting, responding, and resting.

If you're less familiar with this way of praying, you might want to read through my example below of how I engaged with God and this story first. But if you would like to delve straight into this practice, please do so.

1. *Read.* Take some time to silence your heart and your mind, inviting God to lead you in a time of prayer. With a spirit of receptivity and openness, read through Luke 10:38–42 for the first time. (You might wish to play a recording of it to engage your sense of hearing.) During this first step focus on reading to gain an understanding of and familiarity with the story. Ask God to incline your heart and mind toward him, inviting him to impress on you a word or idea from the passage. Read with expectancy and wonder that the God of the universe longs to share his heart with you.

   Looking for a few ideas? Here are some words and phrases that might stand out to you:

   - on their way
   - sat at the Lord's feet
   - listening to him
   - distracted
   - don't you care?
   - left me to do the work
   - tell her!
   - you're worried and upset
   - few things are needed
   - one thing needed
   - the better way
   - won't be taken away

2. *Reflect.* Read Luke 10:38–42 for the second time. During this step ruminate on the text, pondering it as a cow chews its cud. Let the truths sink deeply into your heart, mingling with your thoughts, dreams, and ideas. Turn your prayer into a conversation as you talk through with God what this story means to you as you explore it in more detail. You might want to focus in on Mary sitting at Jesus's feet; or thinking about Martha in the kitchen might resonate with you more. If God revealed a word or image from the story to you in

the first step, focus on that, reflecting on how you relate to it—what does it mean to you? What associations do you have with this word or image?

3. *Respond.* Read the passage a third time, this time giving to God all of the ways you want to respond to him. The word or phrase that stood out to you could act as the doorway in for your response. For example, you might cry out to him for help, asking him to save you from a situation such as too many projects or housework or things to do. You might ask him to give you wisdom and the patience to sit at his feet, learning from him. You might seek courage or strength. Or perhaps you'd like to praise or thank him. Present all of the cries of your heart that the story stirs up in you, trusting that he receives them with joy and love.

4. *Rest.* Read the story a last time, this time focusing on a spirit of rest. Embrace the quiet not only externally but within you—as much as you can. If thoughts pop into your mind that distract you, just ask these thoughts to sit quietly to one side until you are done. You might want to jot them down. Then return to God and rest as you embrace the peace and the sense of well-being he gives.

When you come to the end of the prayer exercise, take a few moments to note what God revealed to you, how you responded, and what you've gained from the experience. You may wish to write down your reflections so that you can revisit them later. I find I can too quickly forget what I feel God gives to me in times of prayer, and these jottings take me right back to the experience of God's grace and love.

## A Snapshot View

To share how simple but deep this practice of prayerful Bible reading can be, here's an example of how I prayed through the Mary and Martha story. In sharing this I'm not suggesting that what God highlighted to me will resonate with you—for instance, I felt led to focus more on Mary than Martha, but you might have a different response. God responds to us as individuals whom he loves dearly and whom he knows intricately. We're his friends whom he cherishes and knows inside and out.

*Read.* Lord, as I read through the story the first time, I ask you please to reveal a word to me. How might you direct me as I engage with this story prayerfully? [I read the passage.] Lord, I really resonate with Martha in the kitchen, but I think you're calling me to focus on "Mary has chosen what is better." Yes, that seems right. Thank you, Lord, for directing me to this phrase from the story.

*Reflect.* Maker of Mary and Martha, I read through the story again and interact with it. [I read the story again.] That phrase "chosen what is better" keeps reverberating within me. Mary chose what is better. I wonder if she felt a pull to the kitchen and all the preparations that needed to be made to feed you, Lord Jesus, and your friends. Did she have to resist the feelings of "should" as she stayed at your feet? I think I would have been in the kitchen already, perhaps stewing along with Martha that, again, all of the work had fallen on me. But Mary had the strength to choose the better way. I'm seeing now that strength of character that Mary had in not joining her sister in the kitchen.

I don't know that I've noticed that before, Lord. I've always been so quick to relate to Martha that I haven't seen what it could have cost Mary to stay at your feet. Perhaps she had to ignore the clattering sounds of vessels being filled and vegetables being chopped in the room next door. Did she have to battle to stay sitting there at your feet? I know I often face distractions in prayer. I can so quickly think of the next thing on my to-do list that I'm tempted to move on to it instead of staying with you.

*Respond.* Loving God, as I read through the story a third time, I can't help but respond to you. [I read the story a third time.] What's your invitation to me as I ponder Mary choosing the better way? How can I train myself to choose when to rest at your feet and when to bustle in the kitchen? I know I get this choice wrong so often. I say yes to kind invitations that affirm me and make me feel needed. And then I have to follow through with them and I get tired and overwhelmed. I said no yesterday, Lord, didn't I. Tiny victories, these are. I loved the sound of that opportunity and know I could have helped her out. But in saying yes, what would I be saying no to? Time watching a movie with my daughter? The freedom of a less-cluttered to-do list? Thank you that you gave me the courage to say no and to do so graciously. Please help me to imbed the practices not only of sitting at your feet but of saying no when I need to.

After all, I know that when I quiet the competing voices in my head and my heart and rest with you, that you refresh me. You give me this strength to say no. You give me insights and help and peace and joy. Your gifts change me, empowering me for when I am ready to do the next thing on my list. I can see how even in the past few days, as this bout of illness keeps me home and forces me to rest, that I haven't turned to you first. Instead I've watched that interior design show or tried to read a book. Nothing wrong with those things, of course, but I want to train myself to choose you first. To find my rest in you. Ah, Lord, I'm remembering that lovely line from Psalm 62: "Yes, my soul, find rest in God; my hope comes from him" (v. 5). As Mary chose what is better, she found rest and hope in you. That's what I want too. I thank you for affirming me and lovingly calling me to a better way. You don't want me exhausted and wrung out. You want me to flourish.

*Rest.* Saving Jesus, I read through the story a fourth time in a spirit of rest. [I read the story a fourth and final time.] I find rest in choosing you. I now will stop my chatter as I spend a few moments sitting at your feet, enjoying your presence.

❦ ❦ ❦

The Lord Is . . .

Jesus is our friend, and a wonderful way to express various aspects of this relationship is through personalizing and adapting Psalm 23. This has been a favorite activity for me since a writer told me about this practice some years ago.[10] I give an example of this practice at the end of each chapter, based on its theme.

Here's my rendition for this chapter, and I invite you to write your own as well.

> The Lord is my colleague, I lack nothing.
>     He makes me a hot drink,
> he leads me to a quiet space for a break,
>     he refreshes my soul.
> He sparks ideas and guides me creatively
>     for his name's sake.

Even though I face
  rejection, hardship, and failure,
I will fear no evil,
  for you are with me;
your tools of the trade,
  they comfort me.
You prepare a desk before me
  in the presence of my critics.
You anoint my hands and head with inspiration;
  my ideas overflow.
Surely your goodness and affirmation will follow me
  all the days of my life,
and I will live with you in your house
  forever.

## Questions for Individual Reflection or Group Discussion

1. As you read through the chapter's overview of this story from Luke, what strikes you? What did you learn that perhaps you'd not come across before?

2. How do you think Martha felt when Jesus told her she was distracted by many things, but not the one necessary thing? How do you think Mary felt as she observed the conversation?

3. How are you wired in terms of work—do you tend toward working too much or not working enough? Why?

4. Jesus said that our work is to believe in the one God sent (John 6:29). What does this mean to you? How are you living this out?

5. When have you felt in partnership with God with a project you've undertaken, whether in the home, community, or workplace? What difference did God's involvement make?

CHAPTER TWO

# Listening and Learning

I sit in the back of the SUV, watching the wipers move rhythmically across the windshield as I pluck up the courage to voice what's deep within. I'm living in the Washington, DC, area, having skipped a semester at my university to continue the internship I'd had as part of a studies program. I've so enjoyed working with Os Guinness and his colleagues that I don't want to go home to Minnesota.

I say to Os and John, "So you know how my friend died in a car accident a couple of years ago? She was only nineteen. Why did a good and loving God allow that to happen? How can I trust God when Sue's life was cut so short?"

With grace, patience, and the willingness to hear my questions, they foster an open and helpful conversation. We talk about the disobedience of Adam and Eve and how God didn't intend the world to exist in this fallen state. About how Jesus, at Lazarus's grave, wept and was angry at the specter of death. About the gift of Jesus as the perfect sacrifice, he who died for our sins and rose to new life, which he shares with us.

I continue to question and probe as we drive back from Os's speaking engagement in Pennsylvania and start to understand that I can voice all of my fears and frustrations to God. I don't have to bury them or hold back, thinking that God can't handle them. Indeed, I understand on a new level that God welcomes a full and frank exploration of what's weighing heavily on my heart. Although I miss Sue so much that I ache, I begin to grasp some of the mysteries of living in a broken world while seeking to trust a good and loving Father.

That period in my early twenties helped to form me and my view of the world. A gift from that time—in addition to the wonderful relationships— was this introduction to thinking deeply. I didn't come to it naturally, and for years afterward, I lacked the confidence to approach matters academically or critically. But working with such thoughtful people helped me desire to gain in wisdom and knowledge. And primarily to know and understand Jesus better.

## Knowing God

Mary longed to know Jesus better, and was willing to buck the cultural forces to do so. In that day, only the male disciples of a rabbi or teacher would sit at their feet. This posture of openness and receptivity would reflect the disciple's humility and the status of someone wiser than them.

Women weren't allowed to be disciples of a rabbi; it just wasn't accepted. Women couldn't even read the Torah, the Hebrew Scriptures, for themselves. In fact, they couldn't even touch them![1] Instead, their husband or their father would instruct them in the Law. Jesus, however, risks the scandal of Mary breaking the cultural norms. Seeing her as worthy of being his friend and disciple, Jesus wants her to learn from him and to sit at his feet (Luke 10:39, 42).

Luke doesn't record what Jesus said as Mary sat at his feet, learning from him, but the Gospels document his sharing with the disciples and crowds how to live and thrive in the kingdom of God. In short, he wanted people to know him and his Father. He would later emphasize this desire during the last long conversation with his friends before he was killed. In a prayer that he prayed aloud so that his friends would hear him, he said to his Father, "Now this is eternal life: that they *know* you, the only true God, and Jesus Christ, whom you have sent" (John 17:3; emphasis added). Jesus wanted them to know his Father and to know him.[2]

Knowing God is a theme throughout the Bible, starting in Genesis when our first parents walked, without regrets and without shame, in the garden with God. They enjoyed sweet intimacy with God. Abraham, the first main leader of God's people, knew God and was called his friend as he weathered hardships and mishaps together with God. Moses, another early leader, shared his longing to know God as he led the Israelites out of Egypt, the land that God promised to them. Moses cried out to God, "If you are pleased with me, teach me your ways so I may know you and continue to find favor with you" (Exodus 33:13). God answered with the assurance to him that his Presence would go with him.

We see the same pattern again and again in the Old Testament as God reveals himself to his wayward, disobedient people. He never gives up on them. And God continues the story in the New Testament. Our Father sent Jesus to live on the earth, and after Jesus died to save us, the Holy Spirit came to live and dwell within God's people.

As we jump to the final book of the Bible, John's Revelation, we delight in God's invitation for us to live with him forever, knowing him and being known by him: "The Spirit and the bride say, 'Come!' And let the one who hears say, 'Come!' Let the one who is thirsty come; and let the one who wishes take the free gift of the water of life" (Revelation 22:17). At the end of our lives here on Earth, we who believe in Jesus will enjoy life together with God for all time. We'll never stop being his friend.

We can presume that Jesus, while staying in Bethany with his friends, taught about himself. He welcomed his followers as friends and wanted them to know him more. And he didn't exclude Mary from the circle of learning but invited her to think and ponder and receive. He honored her desire to open herself up to him as she received his wisdom and grace.

## Jesus the Advocate

As we consider the role of Mary in this story, take a moment to note that she doesn't say anything. We don't get to know her character as much as we do Martha's, and her silence might lead us to think that she passively acquiesces to Jesus's speaking on her behalf. We might also wonder what she's thinking. We don't have the benefit of knowing how Mary responds to Martha's impassioned plea to Jesus, whether she bristles or cowers or looks on her sister with compassion.

We know, however, that Mary chooses to sit at Jesus's feet as she soaks in his teaching and instruction. She's made the decision to be there, not giving in to societal or sisterly pressures and therefore stewing in the kitchen when she'd rather be learning and receiving from Jesus. In her quiet pose she decides how she spends her time.[3] And instead of Mary having to argue her case before either Jesus or Martha, Jesus becomes her advocate. He's not judging her behavior but replying on her behalf.[4]

We can't physically sit at Jesus's feet today, but God knew and planned for that. When Jesus prepared his friends for his impending death, when soon he would leave them, he offered them a promise of hope: "And I will ask the Father, and he will give you another advocate to help you and be with you forever—the Spirit of truth" (John 14:16–17). He spoke of how those who love and obey him will be loved by his Father. And how "the Advocate, the Holy Spirit, whom the Father will send in my name, will teach you all things and will remind you of everything I have said to you" (John 14:23, 26).

Jesus's promises were not only for them at that time, but are for us today. We can look to the Holy Spirit to instruct and guide us into all truth. The Spirit will also be our comforter, another shade of meaning from the original language. And the Spirit of Jesus will act as our advocate in the sense of being a lawyer on our behalf. After all, we need help to stand against the attacks of our enemy, Satan, which means "the accuser." God through his Spirit will lead us into what is right, pure, true, and holy as opposed to believing the father of lies. And the Spirit will convict us when we tell falsehoods or half-truths. Yes, those little white lies that sometimes slip off of our tongues.

## One Thing Needed

Over the years, many thinkers and theologians have grappled with Jesus's words to Martha as he defends Mary in this scene. What, they wonder, does he mean by the one thing needed that Mary chose: "You are worried and upset about many things, but few things are needed—or indeed only one"

(Luke 10:41–42). As we ponder what Jesus said and how these early Christians understood his meaning, we can apply its truth to our own lives. And we can ask Jesus our friend and teacher to enlighten us through the help of the Holy Spirit.

One influential person who addressed this gospel story is Augustine of Hippo, the philosopher who lived at the turn of the fifth century.[5] His comments sound as if they could be written today: "You are busy about many things: Martha's busy-ness has taken possession of you, or rather of us all."[6]

He emphasizes that Mary chose better because she listens to Jesus, the Word who was with God and was God in the beginning (see John 1:1). She's not eating the bread that Martha makes and shares, but rather she's eating and drinking justice and truth: "She was enjoying truth, listening to truth . . . longing for truth."[7] In doing so she's refreshed and nourished by the bread that never diminishes.[8] For Augustine, the better part is choosing Jesus. Although Martha serves Jesus's earthly body, Mary focuses on what will last for all time.

Perhaps the sixth-century bishop Gregory the Great drew on Augustine's commentary when he notes how Christ praised Mary while not condemning Martha.[9] He says how the "works of the active life pass with the body but the joys of the contemplative life become greater after the end."[10] As we live as flesh-and-body beings, we can and should continue to serve others, even though after we die, we'll enjoy truly amazing communion with God.

Other early theologians agree that the "one thing needed" is God—searching for him, pondering him, contemplating him, loving him. For example, the French abbot Bernard of Clairvaux thought the one necessary thing speaks to the eternal unity found between God and Christians, between Christians and fellow believers, and between the Father, the Son, and the Holy Spirit.[11]

We deny ourselves as we combine prayer with action. That is what the author of *The Imitation of Christ*, Thomas à Kempis, and Spanish mystic John of the Cross land on as the main thing.[12] In losing ourselves by serving God we find ourselves (see Matthew 10:39). The third-century scholar and theologian Origen has a similar emphasis, seeing the one thing as the love of our neighbor.[13] When is the last time you chatted with your neighbor?

In summary, these thinkers emphasize that our main focus should be God—he who loves us unendingly and whom we love and adore in response. What's your response? Consider what you think Jesus means when he says that Mary has chosen the one thing necessary. You could spend some time sharing your conclusions with a friend or a small group, or writing them out in a prayer journal, or pondering them while going on a walk. Mull through how God might be inviting you to emulate Mary as you focus on the one thing needed in your life.

## Time to Pray: Sitting at the Feet of Jesus

In Mary's sitting at the feet of Jesus, we can find inspiration and encouragement to move past the cultural and societal expectations we might feel as we embrace the path we discern God leads us on. We might also have to work through fears and discomfort as we follow Mary's example of a bold, wholehearted commitment to live for Jesus and be discipled by him. But we don't do this on our own. Know that God helps us moment by moment in this all-life venture while releasing to us his unlimited resources. One of the ways he might do so is through prayer.

Having examined the narrative from this angle and that, you may be familiar with it on a deeper level intellectually than you were before. Now I invite you to engage with this story with your imagination through prayer. God created us not only as rational beings but as imaginative ones, and we can ask his Holy Spirit to lead and guide us as we pray, and to prevent us from veering off in unhelpful ways.

As you pray with the help of your imagination, God might reveal a truth or an emotion that you might not have been aware of previously—he might bring it to your attention through a side window instead of the front door. God will be your trusted guide as you pray, leading gently and according to his will. You don't need to rush ahead or try to engineer something to happen.

### A Welcoming Space

Quiet yourself and invite the Holy Spirit to lead as he wishes. Know too that God might take you in a direction that is completely surprising. Go with him; he knows all of your needs, cares, desires, hurts, and fears, and his tender love for you means that he wants to shower you with affirmation, healing, and care.

The focus in this time of prayer is calling to mind the truth that as followers of Christ, he dwells within us. As Jesus said to his friends the night before he died, "On that day you will realize that I am in my Father, and you are in me, and I am in you" (John 14:20). We use the story of Mary nestling at the feet of Jesus to help us focus on being, not doing. When we too sit at his feet, we can receive from him as she did. And we too can choose the one thing needed.

Let's begin with a prayer:

> *Lord Jesus Christ, you dwell within those who seek and love you,*
> *who have invited you to live within them. We ask you to baptize our*
> *imaginations, that your Holy Spirit will lead us during this time. Send*
> *away anything that is not of you. Strengthen our love for you and our*
> *ability to discern your voice. May we know how much you love us. You*
> *have called us by name, and we are yours. We pray in the name of Jesus,*
> *amen.*

Breathe deeply a few times, asking God through his Holy Spirit to move throughout your heart, mind, and soul. Welcome him into every cell in your being, his loving presence inhabiting all parts of you—body, spirit, and soul. As you inhale deeply, breathe in the peace of God. Then exhale, releasing any cares that press in on you.

Ask God to make you fully present to his presence in the moment. Pause and enjoy being with him. Perhaps you sense his Spirit, bestowing on you a deep feeling of peace.

## Entering the Scene

Take some time to think about the scene in Bethany—Jesus and his disciples at the home of Martha. She didn't know he was coming, and now she's bustling about, perhaps making a list of what needs to be done, her attention moving from one thing to another as the anxiety builds within her, causing her pain in her stomach. She issues orders and wonders if those working in the kitchen will follow through.

As she thinks about more and more things that need doing, she becomes more and more flustered—and increasingly cross with Mary. She glimpses her sitting at the feet of Jesus. Just sitting there! While she slaves among the pots and pans!

Pause and ask yourself what you think Martha is thinking at that moment. What she's feeling. If you were Martha, what would be going on in your head and your heart?

As you consider Martha, ask God to show you a time when you've been distracted by many things.

Don't go digging for memories; just rest and know that if God wants you to remember something, he'll reveal it to you through his Spirit. If a memory came up, what happened to distract and fluster you? How did you act? Did you respond sinfully? What was driving your response? Spend a few moments asking God to shed some light on that experience. If you need to confess anything to him, do so.

Now take a few moments to look at Mary. There she is, sitting at Jesus's feet. She doesn't mind that she's breaking cultural conventions as a woman who shouldn't be sitting at the feet of a rabbi. Or that her elder sister isn't pleased about her being there. She simply doesn't want to miss out. She wants to soak up Jesus's teaching and receive his love.

Take a few moments to ponder what Mary might be experiencing at that moment. Then consider when you last sat at the feet of Jesus. What led you to do so? What happened in those moments?

Now let's spend some time sitting at the feet of Jesus—this is choosing the better way. You can trust that what Jesus said to the sisters applies to you too, that this won't be taken from you. Picture yourself settling down, crossing your legs without any pain or discomfort as you nestle in close to his robes.

Spend some moments of quiet enjoying his presence. He might teach you, as he taught Mary, or he might lead you differently. Indeed, you might enjoy the quiet together. Know that you don't have to say anything or do anything—you can just be with him, enjoying his presence.

As we bring this exercise to an end, enjoy the promise that Jesus is with us always. You can use your imagination to sit at his feet whenever and wherever you are. Know that he is with you.

Let's close in prayer:

*Loving Jesus, you welcome me to sit at your feet and enjoy your presence. Keep teaching me as you share from your unfailing wisdom. Shower me with your affection and love. Dwell within me, as you promised, so that I may always reflect your love and life to those whom I meet. Amen.*

When you are ready to move from the prayer exercise, take a few minutes to consider what you experienced, and especially if you sensed God working in your life. You might wish to capture what you discerned as coming from God in a prayer journal, through writing or drawing.

❧ ❧ ❧

## The Lord Is . . .

As we've seen in this story while focusing on Mary, Jesus is our everything—the one thing needed, so to speak. But in this adaptation of Psalm 23 I've focused on Jesus being our teacher. Might you pause to pen your own version?

The Lord is my teacher, I lack nothing.
   He makes me rest from my studies,
he leads me beside the bubbling brook,
   he refreshes my soul.
He guides me along the right ways of thinking
   for his name's sake.
Even though I trudge
   through the valley of foggy thinking,
I will fear no evil,
   for you are with me;
Your assignments and comments,
   they comfort me.
You prepare a place for me
   at the academic high table.
You anoint my hands to type;
   my ideas overflow.

> Surely your goodness and love will follow me
>    all the days of my life,
> and I will dwell in the College of the Lord
>    forever.

## Questions for Individual Reflection or Group Discussion

1. When you trace the pattern through the Old Testament and the New of knowing God and being known by him, what strikes you? How do you think God is calling you to know him better?

2. How do you view Jesus? As your friend, advocate, teacher, truth-teller, other?

3. In terms of the early Christians and the "one thing needed," which of them do you agree with most? Augustine and Gregory the Great with their view that Mary chose better because all things will pass away? Bernard of Clairvaux, that eternal life, unity, and the Trinity are key? Thomas à Kempis and John of the Cross on prayer combined with action? Why?

4. In what periods of your life have you felt closest to God? How much of that closeness came from you focusing on the "one thing needed"?

5. What do you think happens when we engage with a gospel story through our imaginations? How does the Holy Spirit aid and guide us in this?

## CHAPTER THREE

# Both . . . And

Some years ago, after writing my first book, I had an online stalker. Wherever I went online—whether on this social-media platform or that one, whether on my website or via email—this person seemed to pop up. She criticized my name, my words and ideas, my writing. I mostly could ignore her, reporting her posts and marking them as spam while pressing delete. Her criticisms felt like the buzzing of a gnat in my ear, continual but—for the most part—harmless. Yet she posed a question that made me take pause: "What qualifications do you have to share these spiritual truths?"

I couldn't answer her because I hadn't had any formal theological training. I'd gained so much over the years of working closely with spiritually wise and learned people, yet my undergraduate degree wasn't in theology but political science.

Her question niggled at me and as I sat with it, I got in touch with a desire that I'd buried deep within me—to study academically and become a spiritual director.[1] I'd long felt called to a life of prayer and to sharing God's goodness through writing, speaking, and leading retreats, but now I wanted to explore more deeply. I decided to apply for a master's degree program at the University of London to study Christian spirituality.

Doing the MA pushed me on many levels, not least my need to learn how to think critically. I had to weigh arguments against each other, drawing contrasts and deciding which position held the most truth. I also felt incredibly stretched because not only had I not decreased my regular writing and speaking commitments but during that period we experienced some family trauma. My calendar was too packed; I had too many deadlines and not enough margin for rest and recreation. To use the common phrase, I was too much like a Martha.

After completing the degree, I took the next couple of years to recover, not setting any big goals. I was too tired to be Mary sitting at the feet of Jesus—I swung the other way into a period of inactivity borne out of exhaustion.

But my dream of becoming a spiritual director didn't die. I led retreats and acted in this role in an informal way, all the while knowing I needed some hands-on, practical training before I could feel qualified. I offered this desire to God, asking him to guide me in its pursuit. And he did.

A series of doors opened amazingly—I secured a last-minute space on a spiritual-director training program along with unexpected financial help from more than one source. I enjoyed the time of learning, which felt joyful and easy, and soon became aligned with an organization as a spiritual director. A small stream of clients approached me in ways that I didn't orchestrate, and as I stepped into the practice of spiritual direction, I felt a rightness within me. My joy at journeying with others, seeking to help them discern the movements of their soul toward God and others, fills me with gratitude.

I share this snippet from my life because it illustrates the push and pull between action and contemplation, between what some Christians would term "workhorse Marthas" or "contemplative Marys." Going after the MA, I leaned too much into action, leaving little time or energy to respond to God as prayerfully as I'd have liked. I had to reset my body and mind in a period of enforced rest. After that, I had the space and passion to discern through prayer my desire to be a spiritual director. As I voiced my dreams to God, I asked for his help to either move forward with this dream or for his diminishing of it within me.

As I prayed, I relinquished my request to God. I waited to see what would emerge but didn't dwell on the question excessively. I could then respond to the invitation that God graciously extended to pursue the dream—he didn't snatch it away just because previously I had overdone things. As I tentatively pushed on each door and found it springing open, I walked through to the next part of the journey. My excitement grew as I felt the partnership with God. I'd ask his advice, offload my questions or concerns, and follow the gentle nudges of his Spirit.

## Opposing Types?

My story of the partnership between spending time with God and serving him is one example of how God might work in a life. I hope that through it you can sense some of the ways we can pray and pursue, wait and relinquish, pause and act with God. It shows how we can veer too much in either direction—morphing into either hyperactivity or the feeling of sloth.

Too often, however, people see action and contemplation as opposing characters or types, with Martha and Mary embodying them respectively. This dichotomy has roots in the writings of some of the early church thinkers, who used the story to illustrate the relationship between praying and doing.[2] This then has spilled over into the modern-day practice of Christians asking if you're a Mary or a Martha. Interestingly, the early church writers were mainly male and applied the story to their lives, but today we seem to interpret it exclusively as being relevant to the lives of women.

So today an overcommitted woman declares "I'm a Martha!" while feeling like a martyr but also not wanting to give up her duties and roles. "Oh, I can't help you, I'm a Mary," another says, shirking a practical task she wants to avoid. Turning two characters from the New Testament into opposing roles can prove suffocating and constricting. Notice how one character and her underlying trait is pitted against the other:

We hear Martha;
We see Mary.[3]

Martha serves Jesus;
Mary receives from Jesus.

Martha works;
Mary sits at leisure.[4]

Martha spends herself;
Mary receives her fill.

Martha's concerned with how she will feed the Lord;
Mary with how the Lord will feed her.[5]

Martha's focused on the laborious and toilsome;
Mary on the restful and blessed.

Martha concerns herself with things of the earth;
Mary concerns herself with things of heaven.

Martha with things that won't last;
Mary with things everlasting.

To continue the juxtaposing images, some see Martha as representing Peter in the Gospels—both characters who live the life of faith, labor, and active work. While in contrast they see Mary representing John—people who inhabit vision, rest and home, and contemplation.[6]

But this typecasting submerges the real person underneath the label. It excludes, for instance, Mary's crisis of faith or Martha's bold profession of faith that we'll explore next in the story of the death of Lazarus. Thus we miss out on the fully orbed person when we turn to an either/or approach. As Origen said, "You might reasonably take Martha to stand for action and Mary for contemplation. . . . [But] there is no action without contemplation, or contemplation without action."[7]

We don't need to pit Martha against Mary or Mary against Martha. Martha isn't bad because she works in the kitchen; neither is Mary a saint because she sits at the feet of Jesus. What's key is that Martha is worried about many things and that Mary has chosen the best thing. We're called to do and be both—that is, we can *be* and we can *do*. We can marry praying with doing.

After all, we need times of quiet listening coupled with times of inspired action. I like how Aelred of Rievaulx, an English monk from the 1100s, stated the relationship between the two: "In no way should you neglect Mary on account of Martha, nor Martha on account of Mary. For if you neglect

Martha, who will feed Jesus? If you neglect Mary, what does it matter that Jesus entered your house, when you taste nothing of his sweetness?"[8]

He cautioned against the kind of typecasting we still see today: "But those who think that some should be Marthas and some should be Marys are making a mistake and do not understand aright. Both these women live in . . . one house; both are pleasing and acceptable to the Lord, both beloved of the Lord."[9] The key here is that God loves both women deeply and calls them to love him most of all.

## False Marthas and Marys

The typing of these women into opposing traits leads to an interesting discussion of so-called false Marys and Marthas—which I hinted at in my opening story as I worked too hard and then collapsed in exhaustion. The conversation about a false Mary or a false Martha started in the twelfth century, when they attributed negative intentions and attitudes to the sisters and how they embraced their roles.[10] Examples of these types help to illustrate.

### Too Much Work

As I shared in chapter 1, I can relate to the description of the false Martha—when she doesn't spend time quietly listening to God, she can become bossy and driven, and over-motivated by results. Perhaps she seeks the approval of others. Ultimately she may find herself disappointed by the level of appreciation she receives or by her own capabilities. She becomes worn out, brittle, and angry.

Not long ago I had a dream that woke me up. I don't often remember my dreams but this one was so vivid that it stayed with me, and I feared I wouldn't get back to sleep.

In the dream I welcomed a guest to our home and for some reason, without our consent, she ended up moving in. She was a burden who drained us as a family. Even worse, she brought four dogs into our home. Four dogs! One of our kids is super allergic, so even one dog would have been harmful. I woke with a feeling of dread deep within, knowing that I'd have to confront and evict her.

I later considered the dream, asking God what it meant. As I prayed I understood that the dream focused my attention on my need to do and to achieve. I needed to ponder whether I was saying yes to too much—were all of my projects and work becoming an unwelcome guest in our home? Were they a visitor who embedded herself with us, not only burdening us but harming the family? As I prayed and pondered, I sought God's help in realigning myself to his way of living.

I needed to heed what I discerned to be a warning about my patterns of work and how too often I'd answer affirmatively when a project presented itself to me or when someone needed help. I'd so equated *doing* for God that I wasn't simply resting and spending time with Jesus. My need to achieve had morphed into an unwelcome house guest whom I had a hard time evicting. Indeed, she still likes to slip through the door when I'm not vigilant.

## Too Much Isolation

A false Mary, in contrast to a false Martha, hides away without serving God and others; she becomes introspective and withdrawn. She might hold back for herself the wisdom she's gleaned from God instead of sharing it with her community.

One of my prayer partners, Ali, resonates with Mary in this story.[11] As she says, "I have always been a contemplative pray-er, and that's partly down to having an introverted nature." Sometimes when she's praying, she likes to sit on the floor by an empty chair, imagining Jesus sitting in the chair with her at his feet. This has "always been a comforting, safe place of prayer" for her. But as she looked back over her life and especially to her early years as a Christian, she realized that "as much as I'm sure that God was pleased I was spending time with him I wasn't always submitted to his will and I didn't always make space for others' input in my life. I had become an isolated pray-er, lacking fellowship."

As Ali grew and matured in her Christian faith, God gently pointed out this deficiency to her. He called her out of her isolation by impressing on her words of encouragement that she could share with other people. As she passed along these verses of Scripture, uplifting messages, and the other gifts she had received in her times with God, she had more and more contact with people. Soon some people sought her out for prayer or to join an intercessory prayer team. As she reflected, "I am a trusted prayer contact for many, and that is an absolute miracle being the personality that I am!"

What I love about Ali's story is how it mirrors her gentle personality and outlook. God honored her and didn't push her into a way of living that she would have found excruciating and draining—such as being responsible for the catering needs at events or for hosting them. He drew her out of isolation into service in ways that help her to flourish while she contributes to his kingdom.

## Too Heavenly Minded for Any Earthly Good

Another story that illustrates this idea of a false Mary—this one being too heavenly minded for any earthly good, as the saying goes—was relayed by one of the desert fathers.[12] A visitor came to see a monk, a revered man of God who lived in community with others. When the visitor saw the brothers working at their daily chores, he said to them with a sniff, "'Do not work for food that spoils,' John 6:27." He added, "'Mary has chosen what is better,' Luke 10:42."

He was shown to a cell and given a book to read, where he spent the day. As his stomach started to gurgle, he wondered why he hadn't been called for the meal. He asked the monk, "Did the brothers eat? Why wasn't I called to join them?"

The monk replied, "Ah, we didn't call you because you are a spiritual man and do not need that kind of food. But we, being carnal, want to eat and that's why we work. But you have chosen the good portion and read the whole the day long and you do not want to eat carnal food."

The story concludes: "Mary needs Martha. It is really thanks to Martha that Mary is praised."[13]

# Life with God

For me, learning how to speak to groups has been a process of growth. During those first engagements, feeling anxious, I'd hide behind a lectern, immersing myself in my notes. To become freer in my speaking, I've come to depend—moment by moment—on my friendship with God and the marriage of prayer and action. When my nerves want to propel me forward to my next point in a flurry, I stop and breathe deeply, reminding myself that God knows these dear people I'm speaking to intimately. He draws me out of myself with his reassurances that he's with me, and the peace he gives to me spills out in what I share. Often when I slow myself down and listen to his promptings, he leads me to share just the right illustration. I can relax knowing that God is with me.

Our friendship with God models to us how to combine being and doing. As we listen to him, hearing his affirmation and sensing his guiding, we grasp that he loves us. We discern his calling to serve in ways that suit our passions and personalities. We give to him our hopes, dreams, and desires as we ask him to lead us into a spacious place where we can flourish.

As we live in an intimate, day-by-day relationship with God, we'll have time to be quiet in his presence and to discover opportunities to serve with love. Through his Spirit, we'll be able to discern where and how we can reach out to others as we honor him. And, importantly, when to rest.

We discover that the promptings of God through his Spirit are the key to marrying action and contemplation. We obey the still, small voice that young Samuel heard as he slept in the Temple.[14] As we stay close to God, we sense when we need to rest and when we should act. Our friendship with Jesus undergirds all we are and all that we do.

## Time to Pray: Looking Back to Move Forward

Let's pray about integrating our being and doing. While reflecting on this theme of action and contemplation, you'll have the opportunity to look back while seeking to move forward with God. Two questions may help focus this time of prayer: What makes you forget or ignore Jesus? Where have you overcommitted yourself?

Praying while looking back to move forward can entail five steps—give thanks, ask, review, repent, renew. You might wish to write out your prayers as you move through each step, or speak them out, or sketch them. If you'd like to go for a prayer walk, I'd recommend noting the steps on your phone or on a slip of paper so that you can refer back to them at various points. If you prefer praying with others to a solitary time, you could talk through the five steps with a trusted prayer partner.

1. *Give thanks.* Turn your heart to God in thanks, sharing with him specific ways that you're grateful. Call to mind times that you have embodied a healthy balance between contemplation and action. Ask God through his Spirit to help you to remember his goodness

in your life, and how he helped you in various situations to rest or to act.

2. *Ask.* Invite God to help you look back over a period of time, asking him to reveal to you where you veered too much into action as you ignored spending time with him, or too much into introspection or withdrawal, not serving others enough. Don't go digging into your memory, but wait with a sense of expectancy. Of course, you might have the balance just right! If so, ask God to help you continue to pray and serve with joy and passion. If not, you might find yourself remembering situations when you were overwhelmed with your to-do list or feeling disconnected and alone.

3. *Review.* If you've landed on a memory of when you over- or under-emphasized prayer or service, review it with God. That is, consider your words, thoughts, and actions and why you responded as you did. Where and when did you move toward God in this area, and why? Where and when did you move away from him? You might wish to jot down the circumstances of the situation, what you felt, and why you acted as you did.

4. *Repent.* Ask God to forgive you for the ways you failed him. Being specific here can help us release the shame and hurt as we seek God's cleansing and release. Don't rush this step as you receive his love, forgiveness, and grace.

5. *Renew.* While conversing with God about all that you've remembered and brought before him, look forward to tomorrow, making plans for how you want to live as a child of God. Commit to living a life of contemplation that fuels action, and a life of action that returns your focus to intercession, petition, giving thanks, and adoration.

🍂 🍂 🍂

## The Lord Is . . .

How does Jesus combine action and contemplation? By being himself. He took times out to pray and to be with his Father, and other times he entered fully into teaching, healing, and sharing the good news. Thus I've focused on Jesus himself in this rendition of Psalm 23 instead of writing about the

Lord as a contemplative activist. Why not give this writing in the form of Psalm 23 a go?

> The Lord is Jesus, I lack nothing.
>     He makes me rest and dwell with him,
> he leads me to places that refresh me deeply,
>     he restores my soul, body, and spirit.
> He guides me in times of quiet and times of action
>     for his glory and honor.
> Even though I walk
>     through excruciating hardship,
> I will fear no evil,
>     for you are with me;
> your bread and your wine,
>     they sustain me.
> You prepare a table before me
>     in the presence of those who hate me.
> You shower me with love and affirmation;
>     your goodness overflows.
> Surely your grace and mercy will accompany me
>     all the days of my life,
> and I will dwell in your mansion with you
>     forever.

## Questions for Individual Reflection or Group Discussion

1.  How do you view action and contemplation, and how do you strike a balance between them? List periods in your life when you were motivated by one or the other, or a combination of both.

2.  In your experience, how often do you speak of, or hear people talk about, being a Mary or a Martha? How do you feel about this commonplace practice now, after you've delved more fully into the story?

3.  Of the list of contrasting images of Mary and Martha on pages 41–42, which, if any, ring true to you? Why or why not?

4. How does a "false Martha" drive herself and others far from Jesus? How can a "false Mary" keep herself from truly encountering God? Which extreme might you more often veer toward, and why?

5. How might you best combine prayer with action in your own life? How is God calling you to increase either your prayer or your action, or both?

## PART 2

# Grieving and Rejoicing

## The John 11 Story

The second account reveals a moment of crisis for Mary and Martha when their brother dies. Grief, disbelief, heartache, and disappointment reverberate through the sisters—as we too experience in life. They send for Jesus but he delays coming. Then both Martha and Mary say the same words to Jesus: "Lord, if you had been here, my brother would not have died" (vv. 21, 32). Yet how they each utter that line differs, which we explore, and what happens next.

# CHAPTER 4

# Waiting for Jesus

**Newly married,** I'm recovering from our whirlwind courtship and wedding, the honeymoon in which I was in bed for all the wrong reasons (with flu), and the move from the Washington, DC, area to Cambridge, England. Feeling a sense of physical and emotional whiplash, I look around the small room in our college accommodation and wonder what to do next. I decide to assemble my desktop computer.[1] After fitting the pieces together, I plug it in and hit the power button with a flourish. But then I hear a whoosh followed by silence. When I examine the computer I notice that I haven't flipped a switch at the back. I can't contain the tears as I realize I've just blown my way to communicate with loved ones in the States.

Well-meaning friends have said that I'll enjoy a honeymoon period in my newly adopted country, but with the computer crash, I sink into despair. When I served at the nonprofit in Washington, my colleagues encouraged me to recognize that my work is not my identity, but I start to realize just how much I've wrapped up who I am with what I do. Now that I'm not working—the diocese will pay our rent for the final six months of Nicholas's theological studies so long as I am not earning income—I wonder just how

I'm supposed to spend my days. With Nicholas off at his class, I'm all alone. I miss my friends and family.

I decide I should bake something, so negotiate riding the new-to-me bicycle on the lefthand side of the road, trying not to get lost while feeling conspicuous about the bike's neon orange and green. *I guess the American who owned it before me liked these garish colors*, I think. Once at the grocery store, I try to figure out what self-rising flour is while looking for the baking powder.

I give up, buying some scones instead. *Why is everything so darn hard in this country?* Back in our flat, I bounce onto the institutional dorm-style couch, forgetting how firm it is, and turn on the television, choosing an old movie from the five available channels. *Is this what my life has become?* I think, holding back my tears. *Where are you, God?* No reply. *More silence, Lord. Thanks a lot.*

## Feeling Abandoned by God

I share that snapshot from my new life in England because those early months—which I had anticipated would be a glorious time of rejoicing with my new husband—left me sad, confused, and seemingly distant from God. For me the most difficult aspect was feeling so far from God that I couldn't hear him. That he'd united me to my husband and invited me to move across the ocean and then abandoned me.

From my previous times of experiencing a "dark night of the soul" when God felt unreachable, I believed that at some point I'd experience the pleasure of his company again. But understanding that in my head didn't stop the ache in my heart. As I negotiated my new life with Nicholas in this foreign land, I longed for God to send me some kind of love note. When I could muster the energy and faith, I asked him to help me to trust and believe that he was with me, even though in my numbness I sensed nothing of his presence.

My despair wasn't at the level of the death of a loved one—I'd felt that when I was nineteen—but I was surprised by my reaction. I had longed to be married, but I hadn't realized that my new partnership would come at such a cost. Or that I'd feel like I'd lost my lifeline to God.

In terms of crisis hotlines to Jesus, Mary and Martha had a direct one, but when they reached out, he didn't answer them right away. As we'll see, they had to wait hour after excruciating hour as they watched their beloved brother descend further into ill health. They probably stared at their door, wondering when the knock would come and Jesus would appear to save Lazarus. But they heard no knock. Lazarus took his last breath. He died.

Why would Jesus abandon them? Join me in digging into the story to explore what might have been behind his silence.

## A Tale of Two Sisters

Note how Lazarus isn't the main subject in this story; rather, he's the object. That is, he becomes sick, he dies, he's put into a grave, he comes out when he's called.[2] We never hear him speak anywhere in the Gospels.

> Now a man named Lazarus was sick. He was from Bethany, the village of Mary and her sister Martha. (This Mary, whose brother Lazarus now lay sick, was the same one who poured perfume on the Lord and wiped his feet with her hair.) So the sisters sent word to Jesus, "Lord, the one you love is sick."
>
> When he heard this, Jesus said, "This sickness will not end in death. No, it is for God's glory so that God's Son may be glorified through it." Now Jesus loved Martha and her sister and Lazarus. So when he heard that Lazarus was sick, he stayed where he was two more days, and then he said to his disciples, "Let us go back to Judea."
>
> "But Rabbi," they said, "a short while ago the Jews there tried to stone you, and yet you are going back?"
>
> Jesus answered, "Are there not twelve hours of daylight? Anyone who walks in the daytime will not stumble, for they see by this world's light. It is when a person walks at night that they stumble, for they have no light."
>
> After he had said this, he went on to tell them, "Our friend Lazarus has fallen asleep; but I am going there to wake him up."
>
> His disciples replied, "Lord, if he sleeps, he will get better."

Jesus had been speaking of his death, but his disciples thought he meant natural sleep.

So then he told them plainly, "Lazarus is dead, and for your sake I am glad I was not there, so that you may believe. But let us go to him."

Then Thomas (also known as Didymus) said to the rest of the disciples, "Let us also go, that we may die with him." (John 11:1–16)

Lazarus's raising from the dead is the second longest narrative in John's gospel (the longest being the story of Jesus's death and resurrection), meaning it's a key passage. John's style is detailed, dramatic, straightforward, and matter-of-fact.[3]

The story is known as the raising of Lazarus, but Jesus performs the miracle at the request of Mary and Martha. So we can also see it as a tale of two sisters, of how they respond to Jesus when their brother dies. It's a snapshot of their grief, of how they pour out their feelings to Jesus, but it also chronicles their faith. It reveals how Jesus brings change in the sisters and in Lazarus.

Jesus's raising of Lazarus is the pinnacle of his seven signs—seven of his miracles that John records to affirm that Jesus is God.[4] John also highlights Jesus's seven "I am" statements—such as "I am the bread of life" (6:35), "I am the light of the world" (8:12), and "I am the good shepherd" (10:11)—to point to Jesus's divinity too. And here, when Jesus says, "I am the resurrection and the life" (11:25), it's the culmination of his seven "I am" sayings. In fact, his miracle fleshes out his "I am" statement—waking up Lazarus from the dead shows how he is the resurrection and the life.[5] It's the last of the seven signs because death is the final enemy that needs to be defeated.[6] Of course, Jesus's death and resurrection is the greatest miracle of all.[7]

Jesus, being both human and divine, knows that the timing of the miracle is crucial. He understands the darkening clouds that have been gathering will burst forth in a raging storm when he performs this miraculous deed. Then the religious opponents will set in motion his crucifixion.[8]

Jesus also reveals his humanity and divinity through being both vulnerable and authoritative, through weeping and defeating death.[9] By the miracle he shows the sisters—and the disciples—that he is the master of life and death.

## The Love of Jesus

"I'm afraid I have some sad news . . ." my sister said over the phone, an ocean separating us. I could feel my heart pounding as I asked, "What's wrong? Is it Mom? Dad?"

Beth had to share that my mom was in the hospital with heart issues. I learned later that after an ablation, she would recover well. But while waiting, I felt so helpless and so far away as I wondered what was going on, how she was, and what would happen next.

You can probably call to mind similar phone calls or messages when someone you love isn't well or has died. As you think back to the experience, the accompanying feelings may come flooding back, such as time slowing down, your body reverberating with anxiety, and a foreboding sense of numbness. Martha and Mary would have experienced these feelings as they sent their message to Jesus.

As the story opens, John tells us that Lazarus is sick, and he's keen to let us know that this is the brother of Mary and Martha—he names them specifically and the town where they live. Earlier we learned that Jesus had been in the town where he'd been baptized, which is about twenty miles from Bethany, or a day's journey on foot (see 10:40).[10] John mentions that this is the Mary who anointed the feet of Jesus, even though he hasn't yet shared that account in his gospel (11:2). John assumes that his readers know what happened not long before Jesus's triumphal journey into Jerusalem, which we commemorate on Palm Sunday.[11]

When Martha and Mary send word to Jesus about Lazarus they don't even name their brother. Such is their intimacy with Jesus that they know that he'll know that it's Lazarus. John underlines the love between this family and Jesus; note how the sisters say, "the one you *love* is sick" (v. 3) and how John reiterates this mutual love: "Now Jesus loved Martha and her sister and Lazarus" (v. 5).

Perhaps John's statement about Jesus loving the siblings underscores that whatever Jesus allows to happen—even the shocking death of Lazarus—he does so with and because of love.[12] He adores this family, and in the original language of Greek, the perfect tense of this verb means that his love is ongoing and continuing.[13] To get a sense of Jesus's love for them, think of your bestest best friend and their love for you, and multiply that times the biggest number you can think of. Jesus loves them with *agape*, the pinnacle of love; the word infers a sense of preference and being chosen.[14] This is the first time that a gospel names Jesus loving anyone in particular.[15]

We might view the close friendship of the siblings and Jesus with a touch of envy, thinking that we'll never have that level of intimacy with him. After all, they got to interact with him in person, and they all died so very many years ago. But what an amazing assurance we have knowing that Jesus rose from the dead and lives even now. And that he chooses us, prefers us, and showers on us as much *agape* love as he did the beloved sisters and brother. God's not hampered by the limitations of time, space, and geography; after all, he's the creator of time, space, and geography. We can be his friend too, and enjoy the closeness with him that they had.

In their message to Jesus, Martha and Mary could press him to come to them, but they don't. Neither do they request that he heal Lazarus.[16] As Augustine observed, it's as if they said to Jesus, "It is enough that you know. For you are not the one that loves and then abandons."[17] Perhaps another reason the sisters don't ask Jesus directly relates to them grasping what it could cost him. They know that the Jewish authorities suspect that Jesus will usurp the leaders' power, and that he will be endangered if he returns to Judea. Previously there in the temple courts, people tried to stone him, but he slipped away (8:59).

## Jesus Delays

Does Jesus go to the siblings right away? No. Being one with the Father, he knows that the time isn't right—even his deep love for Mary and Martha and their request isn't enough to sway him.[18] How often are we so united with God that, if necessary, we can withstand the pressure of one close to us? Jesus was, and he tells his friends that Lazarus's sickness won't end in death, and that it's for the glory of the Father and the Son. No doubt we've experienced periods of silence that feel excruciating at the time, but God may later reveal how he worked during them.

### Staying Longer

In contrast to Jesus, we, when we think we can help someone, often rush to their side—calling the doctor, looking online for causes and remedies, raising money for medical bills, seeking God's help through prayer. Not Jesus:

"So when he heard that Lazarus was sick, he stayed where he was two more days" (11:6). I wonder if Jesus the man struggled with waiting here. Did some part of him want to dash over to Mary and Martha and make everything right? We're not told, but we know that he's fully human.

With each passing hour the sisters must have felt desperately sad. Not only that their brother died—which happened on the day that Jesus received their message—but that their friend let them down. They would have felt unseen. Unheard. This amazing teacher and companion of theirs, one who worked miracles on God's behalf (as Martha would soon declare), seemingly abandoned them in their time of need. They even had to bury their brother without Jesus being there, as the Jewish custom dictated a burial on the day someone died.

One reason that Jesus may have waited to go to Bethany relates to a well-known Jewish belief. They understood that the soul of a dead person would stay around the body for three days in the hopes that it could reenter the body. But once decomposition set in, the soul would leave the area.[19] That Jesus arrived four days after Lazarus's death would reinforce that the miracle came from God. Because after all of that time, Lazarus was well and truly dead.[20]

## Different Standards

In commenting on this passage, the Victorian English preacher Joseph Parker noted that God's standards of measurement differ from ours. When God appears to be slow in his movements, we often become impatient, crying out to him as little children. "We say, 'Speak to us, Lord, or it will be too late,' because we measure time by our standard."[21] Yet, the London pastor continued, when he experienced God's delays, he always found "some greater blessing than I had ventured either to hope or expect." He concluded that we need to let God be God.[22] We simply don't know all that God does.

When we're in the situation of waiting for God, desperately asking Jesus to intervene, we sometimes can hear only a deafening silence. When we feel left out and abandoned by God, we can remind ourselves that God may have a bigger objective in mind. We can ask him to give us the strength to hang on in these times of sorrow and silence. We seek his objectivity—those glimpses of the bigger picture to help us keep on keeping on.

If you are waiting on God, asking for him to move in the life of a loved one or a situation close to your heart, I hope that during any times of silence, you can embrace the goodness of God, trusting that he loves you deeply. This is where we need a community of people who know us and love us, who will hold up our arms when our energy seeps away. We also can look back over our own lives, perhaps through the help of a prayer journal, to trace God's mercy and love as we remind ourselves of his love for us.

## Back to Judea

Some years ago, the phone rang at dinnertime. A colleague called on our family landline, which she never usually used. She bypassed any niceties and said, "Rob passed."

Caught off guard, and still jet-lagged from my recent trip to Florida, I said, "What? Rob *passed*?" I wondered, *Did she mean* died?

"Yes, Rob passed."

"You mean *died*?" I wasn't trying to be obtrusive, but in the flash of the moment as I processed those two words, a whole jumble of emotions surfaced. On one level I was trying to work out what had happened—had Rob Lacey, this favorite author whom I loved to work with as an editor, really died? Deep down I knew the answer was yes, but I so hoped it wasn't true.

On the surface I was annoyed that my colleague couldn't just say what the reality was, that Rob died. Her doing so wouldn't have brought him back, but in that moment I wouldn't have been distracted by a side issue.

Many Christians seem to have a hard time saying *death*, *died*, or *dying*. Perhaps employing a euphemism feels more comfortable than acknowledging the stark truth of a loved one no longer with us. But Christians should be those least afraid of naming the reality. We'll all die. Yet because of Christ's resurrection, those who believe in Jesus will live forever. Death is no longer a hateful foe.[23]

Jesus's disciples also misunderstood. At first Jesus tells them, and note again the intimate term, that their friend Lazarus sleeps (John 11:11). In the New Testament this was a common way to speak of death. When the disciples take Jesus literally, Jesus has to explain that Lazarus has died. In the Greek, the tense is somewhat abrupt and jarring, and it reveals that Jesus has divine knowledge.

Although Jesus knows his final miracle will speed up the proceedings that will bring about his death, he rejoices that the sign will increase the faith and belief of his friends.[24]

After their conversation about sleep and death, Jesus tells his disciples that they will go back to Judea. He doesn't say let's go to Bethany, which was seen as a space for friendship, but rather to the place where danger awaits.[25] In going there, Jesus places the value of Lazarus's life above his own. He embodies what he will later say to his friends on the night before he was killed: "No one has greater love than this, to lay down one's life for one's friends" (15:13 NRSV).[26] He exemplifies his sacrificial friendship.

When his disciples protest about going there, he shares a short parable about light and darkness. His friends would have remembered Jesus saying that he's the light of the world, so they would have understood his meaning—that when they stick with him, they won't stumble.[27]

## Time to Pray: Praying with the Psalms

We pause at the end of this chapter and adopt, like Mary and Martha, a stance of waiting. Often when we feel distant from God, the last thing we want to do is pray. We don't have any words to offer to God, our silence seemingly matching his. When this happens, we can use the prayer book in the Bible—the Psalms—to help us speak to God.

We can use a psalm as a jumping-off point, as I've done here, with Psalm 27 (which I've modified for our purposes). I invite you to pray along with me, adapting the responses to your own voice.

*Lord, you're my light and my salvation—I won't fear anyone.*
*Lord, you're my refuge—who or what can make me afraid? (v. 1).*

Lord, I do fear though. I can find lots of things to be anxious about, as you well know! I'm afraid of what's ahead of me, of [add any specifics, whether people important to you, situations in your life, national or international concerns]. But, Lord, I want to echo with David that you're my light and my salvation. I want to be able to say, I won't fear as I wait. Help me to affirm that with my whole being, even if I feel far from able to do so.

*When the wicked advance against me or horrible things happen,*
*my heart won't fear. Even if war breaks out against me, I'll still be*
*confident (vv. 2–3).*

Lord, I need you to change what's happening because I feel so helpless and hopeless. All that I've worked for—all I've poured my time and energy into—is slipping away. You're silent, Lord. I can't hear you. I don't know if I can join David in saying that my heart won't fear.

Mostly, Lord, I feel shut down and numb. If I allow myself to feel, a flood of emotions will spill out. I will crack wide open and I'll lose control. I'm afraid of that, God. I'm so afraid. Too many feelings. Too much hurt. Too many fears rushing at me.

Lord, why? Why has this happened? Why have you allowed it? Why haven't you changed things? What did I do to cause this to happen?

Oh Lord, I know I'm spiraling down an unhealthy train of thought when I go back again and again to try to figure out why. Help me please to stop that vicious cycle. Help me somehow to put my trust in you, even in this fog of silence.

*One thing I ask from you, Lord; this I seek—that I will dwell in your*
*house all of my days. That I'll gaze on your beauty and seek you in your*
*house (v. 4).*

Lord, it's awfully hard to say that I want to spend all my days in your house. To be honest, I don't know what that looks like. But I want to want this. Please change my heart and warm me up, as I'm so chilled because of your silence. I'm scared that you won't ever speak to me again. Lord, I want to live in your house. I want to cozy up with you, to feel your embrace, to know that I belong and that you love me and will never stop. Show me your beauty, that I will believe.

*In the day of trouble, you keep me safe in your dwelling. You hide me in*
*the shelter of your sacred place. I'll be above the enemies who surround*
*me as I sing and make music to you, Lord (vv. 5–6).*

Lord, you know how much I dislike conflict! It makes me feel all jumbled up inside. I might be itching for a fight, or I become indignant at the injustices I experience or witness. I seem either to run from the conflict or toward it, and so often I try to figure everything out on my own.

Help me to look to you, Lord, and to be like David, confident in you. Help me not to fear the worst. I want to put my trust in you, God; please, help me put my trust in you. Keep me safe in your dwelling, Lord. Surround me with your love and your life.

> *Hear me when I call, God! Show me mercy and answer me. Please, Lord; answer me. My heart says, "Seek your face!" Your face, Lord, I'll seek (vv. 7–8).*

I don't know if I even dare cry out, asking for you to hear me. Are you there? I need you to hear me when I call. I need you to show mercy and to answer me. Please, Lord, I beg you to answer. I want to say that I seek your face, but it's so difficult to do when you're so silent. But I will join David and say that it's your face I seek. I seek your face.

> *Don't hide your face from me. Don't turn me away in anger. You've been my helper! Don't reject me or forsake me, God my Savior. Though my parents reject me, I know that you, Lord, will receive me (vv. 9–10).*

God, don't hide your face from me and don't turn away in anger. I feel so far from you, and if you're angry at me, I won't be able to cope. Don't reject me like the ones who are supposed to love me reject me. I know that you'll receive me, Lord.

> *Teach me your way, Lord. Lead me in a straight path. Don't turn me over to the desire of those who oppose me, to those who spread malicious lies and accusations about me. I'm confident of this—I'll see God's goodness in the land of the living (vv. 11–13).*

Teach me, Lord; lead me in the way I should go. Save me from those who want me to lose and fail, from those who gossip about me and spread horrible lies and half-truths. I believe—at least I want to believe—that I'll see your goodness. You'll reveal yourself, won't you?

*Wait for the Lord. Be strong and take heart and wait for the Lord (v. 14).*

My soul finds peace as I echo David: Wait for the Lord. Be strong. Take heart. And wait for the Lord. Wait, my soul. Wait. Wait for God.

I need to remind myself this again and again—wait for God. Take heart; don't give up; be strong; and wait.

Amen—let it be so.

❦ ❦ ❦

The Lord Is . . .

We might feel that we're living through a dark night of the soul, when God's love seems only a hazy memory. But the Lord is our friend and companion, even when we have to endure the silence. I invite you to craft a psalm in the style of Psalm 23 from the point of view of waiting. Here's mine:

> The Lord is my companion, I lack nothing.
>    He helps me rest when I'm grieving,
> he leads me to quiet waters when I ache and wait,
>    he refreshes my soul.
> He guides me in ways that bring me clarity and relief
>    for his name's sake.
> Even though I walk
>    through times of deafening silence and confusion,
> I will fear no evil,
>    for you are with me;
> your still, small voice and living words of Scripture,
>    they sustain me.
> You prepare a table before me
>    even when my loved one isn't here.

You enfold me in your loving embrace;
    I exude your grace.
Surely your goodness and tenderness will accompany me
    all the days of my life,
and I will live with you and your Father
    forever.

## Questions for Individual Reflection or Group Discussion

1. How do you see the human and divine sides of Jesus through this story? How does your faith develop and grow when you consider Jesus in this light?

2. Why do you think Jesus waited to go to his friends? How do you think he felt in doing so?

3. Jesus loves this family, and yet allows Lazarus to die. How do you make sense of this paradox? Have you felt abandoned by God, and if so, how did you react?

4. Consider and discuss the quotation from Joseph Parker: "Yet Jesus Christ delayed. God does appear sometimes to be slow in his movements. Our impatience cries for him, as he sits still, as if we were but noisy children, not knowing what we were talking about. We say, 'Speak to us, Lord, or it will be too late,' because we measure time by our standard. But God takes his times from something higher than our standards."[28]

5. How do you speak about death? Are you comfortable using the word *death*, or do you prefer a softer substitute? Why?

# CHAPTER 5

# Aftermath

**I'm upstairs in the living room,** unable to sleep. It's only been a couple of hours since I arrived home from the Minnesota Orchestra, but time seems altered. I keep replaying what happened. I think of being surprised to see the light on when I went downstairs to my room—my parents are usually so good at turning off the lights. And how I saw my mom, her eyes red with tears, and her news that shifted my world forever.

*How can Sue be dead?* I wonder. I had screamed when my mom shared what happened, that Sue had been killed in a car accident in Duluth. *She's only nineteen,* I think. *Was nineteen,* I correct myself. *God, how can one of my closest friends be dead? How could you let this happen?*

My mom held me as we cried, then after a while when I said I'd be all right, she went upstairs to get some sleep. But I'm not all right, and sleep won't come as I alternate between sobbing and feeling numb. I think about Sue, who lit up a room with her smile. Memories come to mind as I remember our times together skiing, waterskiing, and swimming off her dock. Of how she loved to tease me about our double date with Tom and Lonnie. How she helped me with physics, her mind so quick and smart.

*And now she's dead. God, what were you thinking!? I can't handle a world without her in it!*

Before coming upstairs I had grabbed a Bible, and now I page through it, the words blurry. *Lord, I'm in so much pain, and I just don't know if Sue is with you or not. Did she love you? I can't bear the thought of never, ever seeing her again. Please show me something. Please, God. I'm desperate.*

As I turn the pages, I stop in 1 Corinthians, and the words come into view: "For who knows a person's thoughts except their own spirit within them? In the same way no one knows the thoughts of God except the Spirit of God" (2:11).

I gasp: *God, how could you lead me to just the right place in the Bible? You're right—I just can't know Sue's thoughts. I am not the judge. Thank you for this gift.*

Somehow I manage to drop off to sleep. I wake, enjoying my dream that Sue and I are watching a movie at her house. But in a flash my joy evaporates when I remember the reality—never again will I hang out with Sue at her house. I sob, scarcely believing it can be true.

These decades later, as I look back on my nineteen-year-old self, I remain profoundly grateful to God for that assurance from Paul's letter to the Corinthians. In the days and months after Sue died, I had many desperate moments of grief and pain, but I knew I didn't need to torture myself over whether or not she was in heaven. Instead, my cries were more along the lines of, *Why, God? Why did she have to die? Why didn't you do something?* Sentiments, I imagine, that may have been voiced by Martha and Mary to Jesus.

## Where Were You?

It's four days since Lazarus died and was buried, and Jesus meets the sisters outside of their home in Bethany. The women handle their grief differently. Again Martha says more than Mary, but Mary does speak—this is the only place in the Gospels that we hear anything from her.

Jesus shows deep compassion and love for these sisters, who in that culture with their brother's death would be worse off than widows. Widows, unlike Mary and Martha, would have their husband's family to support them.

On his arrival, Jesus found that Lazarus had already been in the tomb for four days. Now Bethany was less than two miles from Jerusalem, and many Jews had come to Martha and Mary to comfort them in the loss of their brother. When Martha heard that Jesus was coming, she went out to meet him, but Mary stayed at home.

"Lord," Martha said to Jesus, "if you had been here, my brother would not have died. But I know that even now God will give you whatever you ask."

Jesus said to her, "Your brother will rise again."

Martha answered, "I know he will rise again in the resurrection at the last day."

Jesus said to her, "I am the resurrection and the life. The one who believes in me will live, even though they die; and whoever lives by believing in me will never die. Do you believe this?"

"Yes, Lord," she replied, "I believe that you are the Messiah, the Son of God, who is to come into the world."

After she had said this, she went back and called her sister Mary aside. "The Teacher is here," she said, "and is asking for you." When Mary heard this, she got up quickly and went to him. Now Jesus had not yet entered the village, but was still at the place where Martha had met him. When the Jews who had been with Mary in the house, comforting her, noticed how quickly she got up and went out, they followed her, supposing she was going to the tomb to mourn there.

When Mary reached the place where Jesus was and saw him, she fell at his feet and said, "Lord, if you had been here, my brother would not have died."

When Jesus saw her weeping, and the Jews who had come along with her also weeping, he was deeply moved in spirit and troubled. "Where have you laid him?" he asked.

"Come and see, Lord," they replied.

Jesus wept.

Then the Jews said, "See how he loved him!"

But some of them said, "Could not he who opened the eyes of the blind man have kept this man from dying?" (John 11:17–37)

# Woman of Faith

As we launch into the story, we could overlook the significance of John mentioning the many Jews who came to grieve with the sisters. As a way to explain their presence, he reminds the reader of the close proximity of Bethany to Jerusalem. In his account this term, "the Jews," often signifies those who oppose Jesus. Perhaps John implies that although they offer Martha and Mary comfort, yet they're hostile to Jesus.[1]

In that culture, those grieving wouldn't leave their homes the first week after the burial of their loved ones.[2] And the visiting mourners would stay fairly long—after all, grief doesn't just magically disappear after a certain amount of time. They would seek to bring comfort, which in Greek means "speak by the side of." To do so, the mourners would respectfully say aloud the name of Lazarus to the sisters, each person lamenting his death.[3]

What a contrast to the way we often handle the grief of others! Many people feel awkward in talking to friends or acquaintances whose loved ones have died, thinking that speaking of the person will be difficult for the one grieving. A friend whose husband recently died said to me, "I'm thinking about him all the time anyway, so yes, please say his name."

## Trusting Jesus amid the Pain

Grief can affect people differently, perhaps reflecting their character. Notice how Martha, our can-do woman, springs into action while Mary remains seated in the house (11:20).[4] In the Greek, she *sat* at home—she remained still in her sadness and pain.[5] Perhaps her grief felt paralyzing.

When Martha reaches Jesus, she states the obvious: "Lord! If you had been here, my brother would not have died" (v. 21). Her subtext is, *What were you doing? Why weren't you here?* Yet she follows it up with a statement of faith: "But I know that even now God will give you whatever you ask" (v. 22). Martha trusts that Jesus knows best. She doesn't demand, *Bring my brother back to life!* Rather, she expresses faith in him.[6]

When Jesus says that her brother will rise again, she responds in the wisdom of the Jewish people then: "I know he will rise again in the resurrection at the last day" (v. 24). In speaking of the "last day," she refers to God's promises in the Old Testament: "In the last days the mountain of the LORD's temple will be established as the highest of the mountains; it will be exalted above the hills, and all nations will stream to it" (Isaiah 2:2 and Micah 4:1).

## The Messiah

What she says indicates that Martha thinks of Jesus as a miracle worker—someone who hears from God and does miracles on his behalf.[7] But Jesus wants her to understand that *he's* the one who saves. He makes the pinnacle of the "I am" statements, that he's the resurrection and the life and that all who believe in him will live, even though they die (John 11:25–26). *Zoe*, the word for life in the Greek, means "removed from the power of death."

Jesus, underlining the importance of his statement, asks her, "Do you believe this?" (v. 26). And she answers yes in faith, that he's the Messiah who has come into the world. Hers is an amazing confession of faith, just as Peter in Caesarea Philippi confesses that Jesus is the Messiah. Martha's declaration anticipates what John later says is the purpose of the gospel: "But these are written that you may believe that Jesus is the Messiah, the Son of God, and that by believing you may have life in his name" (20:31).[8]

The interaction between Jesus and Martha demonstrates how when we converse with him, he takes our limited understanding and expands it. Although we can only see the here and now, he helps us to grasp the bigger picture to discern truths that would normally be out of our reach.

I hope that as you consider Martha, you can view her more broadly than only someone who works and serves. She whom Jesus lovingly chastised in the Luke passage now shines as a witness to who Jesus really is. So if someone asks me if I'm a "Martha," I'll be tempted to say with a smile, "Why yes! Like her I believe that Jesus is the Messiah, the Son of God who came into the world."

# In Despair

Martha's love for her sister shines as she goes back to Mary and tells her to go see Jesus—he's asking for her (11:28). Jesus remains outside of the village while he waits for her. He's aware of the controversy his very presence will stir and likely doesn't want to attract too much attention.[9]

Martha now serves Mary; she's no longer frustrated about her spending too much time with Jesus. While during the last interaction, Martha tried to call Mary away from Jesus, here she beckons her sister to him.[10] We see Jesus's love for Mary too, as he wants to comfort her. He knows that she's feeling lost and bereft.

Mary, filled with purpose, rises quickly and goes out to meet him (v. 29). The mourners follow her, and in doing so will become witnesses to his prayer and the miracle that follows (v. 31).[11] Those opposed to Jesus will see with their own eyes that He, the source of life, brings resurrection.

As Mary reaches Jesus, she falls at his feet (v. 32). Up until this point in the gospel, the only one who fell at his feet was the man born blind (see 9:35–38). Interestingly, each time we see Mary in the Gospels, she's at Jesus's feet—first in learning from him (Luke 10:39), now in despairing over the death of her brother (John 11:32), and later in anointing him with precious oil (12:3).

When Mary gets to Jesus she says the same words that Martha said: "Lord, if you had been here, my brother would not have died" (11:32). But her inflection differs from that of her sister. While Martha is more direct and somewhat matter-of-fact, Mary sounds defeated.[12] In the original language, her weeping has the sense of wailing and crying (v. 33).[13] It's a desperate type of crying that reflects a lack of hope and faith. Mary has reached a point of despair.

Even as we can be too harsh with Martha in our Christian culture, we can also overly laud Mary as the saint who sits at Jesus's feet as we overlook this loss of faith. Unlike Martha who shares her grief with Jesus but then confesses him to be the Messiah, Mary makes no such declaration. She gives herself over to her all-consuming sorrow in Jesus's presence—which we are invited to do as well.[14]

## A God Who Mourns

Jesus, as he witnesses Mary's grief and that of the mourners, is deeply moved in his spirit (v. 33). The word in Greek for Jesus's groans reflects an animal snorting—like a horse in times of war or one who races. The meaning involves outrage, fury, and anger.[15] Not only is Jesus concerned for Mary, but he's probably angry at the sin and unbelief that will send him to the cross.

And then we come to that famously shortest verse in the Bible in which Jesus weeps (v. 35). In Greek the word contrasts to that used for the loud and demonstrative crying of Mary and the mourners.[16] Here it's not a loud wailing but an indication of deep grief—such as bursting into tears would express.[17] As the English preacher Charles Spurgeon observed, Jesus's heart churned in a great storm that didn't result in a word of terror or a glance of judgment but simply "a blessed shower of tears."[18]

We have a God who weeps. Jesus shares the grief of his dear friends. His love was evident—the Jews say, "See how he loved him!" (v. 36). Jesus's love for these siblings reverberates throughout him, and his body reacts with tears and grief.

As you consider this story, note how Jesus responds to Mary differently than he does to Martha. He knows the human heart, and instead of entering into a dialogue with Mary, teaching her, he sympathizes with her and takes action.[19] Here theologian David Ford makes a striking observation, that with Martha, Jesus shares meaning through his words. With Mary, in contrast, Jesus is meaning incarnate. "The Word is vulnerable flesh . . . and weeps."[20] Jesus the Word embodies grace to the sisters in individual ways, just as he does with us.

Seeing Jesus weep, some of the Jews note how much he loves Lazarus. But others seem to disdain him, wondering why, if he could heal the blind man, he doesn't prevent Lazarus's death (v. 37). Clearly God will always have detractors; we often will too. When we show emotion or do an act of kindness, we can often be misunderstood or even ridiculed. In these times, we can look to Jesus for affirmation and love, finding strength from our friendship with him.

## Walking with Jesus

After Sue's death turned my world upside down, I tried to numb the pain with work. I threw myself into my university studies and my part-time job, filling my hours with as much activity as I could handle to numb my sadness. I hadn't yet learned how to give my anguish to Jesus, sitting with him and letting the emotions rise to the surface. To do so felt scary—like I would lose control and not stop crying.

Building a friendship with Jesus over many years has helped me turn to him when I'm hurting, disappointed, or feeling sad. The way he brings me peace and grace when I quiet the competing voices builds my faith and makes me want to approach him right away whenever I face trouble.

A more recent example of walking with Jesus during a time of grief was a few years ago, when Nicholas's mother died unexpectedly. Some family conflicts and other issues built up in him and resulted in a season of anxiety and depression, and he was signed off of work.[21] I felt the pressure of wanting to be strong emotionally for not only him but the children too while trying to keep up with my various commitments. All during December, one of the busiest months of the year.

My times of reading the Bible and praying each morning felt like the food that kept me going as I poured out my prayers to God, sharing with him all of my angst, pain, and frustration while I looked to him for help and strength. I continued the conversation throughout the day, but knew I needed those more formal times of prayer each morning to strengthen and encourage me for what I faced. I didn't have any big revelations from God during that season but felt carried and cared for, not only by God but through the hands-on love of some close friends. His—and their—friendship sustained me.

## Time to Pray: Learning to Lament

As we move to our time of prayer, I welcome you to sit with the feelings of sadness and pain that Mary and Martha would have been feeling, even after their friend returns. Try to imagine that you don't know the ending to their story.

### Four Steps

Again we can use the form of a psalm to aid our prayers, this time as we cry out to God in a lament. We'll follow the pattern of Psalm 22.[22] In that psalm and others, David addresses God in four stages:

1. address
2. complaint
3. request
4. expression of trust

David addresses God directly and intimately, he presents his complaint specifically, he makes his request to God, and then he affirms how he trusts in the Lord. Using this fourfold pattern gives us a boundary to our lament. We're free to express all of our pain to God, but we also acknowledge his good character.

Spend some time lamenting. You could start straight in with writing a lament using the four suggested steps as I outline below, or you could go out for a walk with them noted on your phone or on a scrap of paper. My example of a lament based on this story also follows.

*Address.* Begin with prayer, asking God through his Spirit to help you to share what's in your head and heart. As you begin, address God, speaking directly to him. Perhaps you could use one of his titles—does it feel comfortable to call him the Lord of Lords or the King of Kings? You could say Heavenly Father, Almighty God, Creator and Maker.

*Complaint.* Share with God what you find wrong and wanting. It could be something in your life, in your community, in the nation or around the world. Perhaps you want to name a betrayal, or someone sinning against you, or institutionalized evil, or disease and sickness, or the separation you endure from loved ones.

*Request.* Move from complaint to request. Even if you don't feel you have enough faith to believe God will answer, put your request before him. You might, for instance, ask God to address the evil. To make right what is wrong. To heal, comfort, unsettle. Name your request, how you want God to act.

*Expression of trust.* Express your faith in God. You may not feel like you trust him, but you can educate your feelings. You can affirm: "I will trust in you. My heart will rejoice. I will find peace and contentment in your house. I will sing to the Lord, for he is good."

## An Example of Lament

Jesus, both Martha and Mary came to you and they said, Lord, if you'd been here . . . if only you'd been here, he wouldn't have died. But Lord! He died! Jesus, if you'd been here, we wouldn't have lost our brother. Our beloved brother. And now we are bereft; now we will be outcasts. You weren't here. You say you love us, but you weren't here.

Why?

Why?

Why?

But Jesus, you wept at the tomb of Lazarus. You wept in grief and in anger. You came from your Father and you know that the world—our beautiful, broken world—is not supposed to be like this.

Our first parents betrayed you, and now we have death. And now we have sickness. And now we have deception and discrimination and pain.

We pour out our feelings to you. We pour out our lament. We see you at the tomb, weeping.

I know you're faithful, Lord. I may not feel that you are just right now, but I know by my beliefs that you are. And so I ask you to listen. Don't turn your face from me. I can pour out our bewilderment to you. About what is wrong in the world and about what is wrong with me.

You hear me. You know me. You weep too for what is going on. The slights, the pain, the anger, the rejection. Strife between spouses, sons and daughters, sisters and brothers. Hurts that fester and turn into all-out rejection and war. Long-held resentments that never seem to heal.

Come, Lord Jesus, come. Bring resurrection in my life—in whatever is on my heart. That relationship, that project, that buried dream. Bring resurrection.

But as I wait, give me hope. Let me pour out my feelings to you. Help me to express what's deep within.

For you are a good God, loving and kind, merciful and true. I will trust you, my God, all my days. I will trust.

❧ ❧ ❧

The Lord Is . . .

We can join Martha in proclaiming that Jesus is our Messiah. What does that mean to you? Again I welcome you to write out how the Lord is your Savior through the format of Psalm 23. Here's mine:

> The Lord is the Messiah, I lack nothing.
>     He calms me when I'm in deep pain,
>   he leads me to a quiet, restorative place,
>       he brings peace to my anxious soul.
>   He guides me to make wise decisions
>       for his praise and honor.

Even though I walk
    through grief, loss, pain, and sadness,
I will fear no evil,
    for you are with me;
your crook and your cross,
    they sustain me.
You prepare a feast before me
    in the presence of those who scorn me.
You anoint me with healing oil;
    your love washes over me.
Surely your saving love will accompany me
    all the days of my life,
and I will live with you in your comforting home
    forever.

## Questions for Individual Reflection or Group Discussion

1. Compare and contrast how people grieved the death of a loved one in the ancient Near East compared with your culture. What are the pros and cons of each?

2. How does your view of Martha shift from the Luke 10 passage to what we see here? Your view of Mary?

3. How does Jesus meet each of the sisters and minister to them? How does he meet you in your moments of grief?

4. Consider how Jesus brings about transformation in both of the sisters. What strikes you about this change in each of them?

5. Ponder and consider these statements: Because Jesus is the life, he is the resurrection.[23] And, where Jesus is, there can be no death.[24] What do these truths mean to you?

# CHAPTER 6

# At the Tomb

I check the flight tracker and groan when I see that I have four hours and fifty-three minutes left until we land outside of Washington, DC. I sigh, wondering how I'll cope for that long. *Can't think about that now,* I muse. *Just make it through the next few minutes.* I bend down to pick up Baby Elmo from the who-knows-what's-been-on-this floor, giving the beloved companion to my two-year-old daughter, before getting a snack for my five-year-old son. We've been traveling for hours, having left our home in North London early in the morning. After arriving at Dulles Airport and going through immigration, we'll change planes to head to Florida. I try not to think about needing to lug the suitcases, car seats, and all the stuff I seem to need while traveling on my own with two small children.

I check the flight tracker again and see that we have four hours and forty-nine minutes left. With a sigh I turn off the screen completely. *I don't need that kind of discouragement.*

For the next hours I alternate between marveling at my amazing kids for being good travelers while feeling the exhaustion of trying to keep them content and not bothering the passengers around us. Finally, hours and hours later, and with no big meltdowns—either the kids or me—we land in Fort Lauderdale. I gather up the stuff from around us and in the overhead bins. *At least we've already gone through customs.*

I say to the kids, "How excited are you to see Grandma and Grandpa?" My son shouts, "Yes!" and my daughter sports a huge smile and waves her hands. I know that in just a matter of a few moments, the hassles of travel will be worth it. And that my parents will help carry our stuff to the car.

As I walk into baggage claim I scan the carousel where our suitcases will arrive, looking for the familiar faces. I gasp and am tempted to let go of the stroller and my carry-on when I see not only my parents but my sister too. "Beth! What are you doing here?!"

"I thought I'd surprise you!" she says with a smile.

"Oh my goodness I can't believe it! And you all kept it quiet!" I said, looking at my parents. "Best surprise ever."

I release a deep sigh of gratitude, knowing that I will enjoy precious time with my family at the beach before Nicholas joins us. And that I don't have to carry all of the luggage to the car on my own.

## Amazing Grace

All these years later, that story of seeing my sister at baggage claim still makes me smile. I remember so clearly the feeling of relief and joy—the release of being able to share the childcare along with the amazement and wonder I felt that my sister unexpectedly came to Florida.

I share the story because as I think about Lazarus and the tomb, I can't recount how God raised someone from the dead, and I'm guessing you can't either. But no doubt we've all experienced times of unexpected and unadulterated joy, as Mary and Martha felt when their brother walked out of the tomb.

Let's continue with this story of grief, betrayal, death, and the unlikely resurrection:

> Jesus, once more deeply moved, came to the tomb. It was a cave with a stone laid across the entrance. "Take away the stone," he said.

"But, Lord," said Martha, the sister of the dead man, "by this time there is a bad odor, for he has been there four days."

Then Jesus said, "Did I not tell you that if you believe, you will see the glory of God?"

So they took away the stone. Then Jesus looked up and said, "Father, I thank you that you have heard me. I knew that you always hear me, but I said this for the benefit of the people standing here, that they may believe that you sent me."

When he had said this, Jesus called in a loud voice, "Lazarus, come out!" The dead man came out, his hands and feet wrapped with strips of linen, and a cloth around his face.

Jesus said to them, "Take off the grave clothes and let him go."

Therefore many of the Jews who had come to visit Mary, and had seen what Jesus did, believed in him. But some of them went to the Pharisees and told them what Jesus had done. (John 11:38–46)

Jesus again is deeply moved—he's "shuddering," which conveys a vivid image (v. 38).[1] He bellows with rage and grief over the death of his friend.[2] As both God and man, he feels emotions deeply. And he who has the power to move mountains yet asks for the stone to be rolled away (v. 39). One reason may be that if he moves it, those suspicious of him could accuse him of trickery.[3]

Practical Martha is alarmed. The King James Version of the Bible conveys so much of her spirit and forthrightness: "Lord, he stinketh!" (v. 39). Her down-to-earth comment also reminds us of the stench of death—the stink of mortality and evil; the sin and rottenness of decay.[4] She might also be voicing her sense of foreboding and embarrassment as the sister of the dead man; for Jewish people, opening the tomb and coming into contact with the dead would make someone unclean. I imagine she didn't want that sense of responsibility and the accompanying shame.[5]

Martha states more of the obvious—Lazarus has been dead four days (v. 39).[6] She doesn't need to remind Jesus of this all-too-evident reality, but her fears and unbelief propel her to do so. Her recent interaction with Jesus reveals faith in him, but her comment shows that she doesn't yet believe in his power to give life.[7] Jesus, filled with grace, not judgment, reminds her that if she believes, she'll see the glory of God.

## Master of Life and Death

As they roll away the stone, Jesus prays (vv. 41–42).[8] Often when Jesus prays aloud he does so for the benefit of those around him. This time is no exception, as not only the sisters will hear his faith-filled prayer, but the unbelieving Jews and other onlookers will too. Note how Jesus doesn't even ask the Father for anything—rather he thanks God for hearing him (v. 41). Perhaps Jesus started praying about Lazarus as soon as he received the sisters' message, before he arrived in Bethany.[9] Jesus knows that the Father will respond as a sign of his love and favor.

But why did Lazarus have to die? We simply don't know. But Jesus grants free reign to the grave, allowing for death to "seize his friend, drag him down to the underworld, and take possession of him," in the words of a fourth-century Christian, Peter Chrysologus (rather wonderfully known as Peter the Golden-Worded).[10] Jesus allows for the stench of death to spread among the sisters and their community. He permits this depth of desolation and anguish so that all will know that the living God, and not some miracle worker, raised Lazarus from the dead.

With Jesus granting death to do its full work, those who love Lazarus suffer—just as we experience excruciating pain when someone we love dies. But even in these times, we can trust that God loves us and wants the best for us. God can expand our faith in him as we turn to him in our anguish and pain.

In the months after our second miscarriage, which happened days after the death of my friend Rob Lacey, whom I mentioned in chapter 4, Nicholas and I felt a pervading sense of sadness. We also wondered if we should be content with one child. During this period of angst and the sleeplessness we endured with a toddler who wouldn't stay in his bed at night, I kept bringing my feelings and desires to God. Questioning him, asking him, placing my trust in him—if not always fully, then seeking his strength to trust him even when we faced miscarriages and death and very disrupted sleep.

God wasn't napping on the night watch.[11] God through his Spirit comforted us during those broken nights as we returned our son to his bed again and again. And he planted seeds of hope—one of which came to life less than a year later with the birth of our healthy, beautiful daughter. Nicholas and I would endure other hardships and seemingly unanswered prayers in the months and years that followed, but during that season I sought to remember God's mercy in granting life amid a time of sadness and pain.

## Love in Action

We move to the amazing miracle itself. After praying, with a loud voice Jesus calls Lazarus—whose name means "helped"—out from the tomb (v. 43). Here Jesus's reverberating cry contrasts the quietness in which he performed the other miracles considered signs in John's gospel. Note that Jesus also cries out in a loud voice just before he dies on the cross.[12]

Jesus names Lazarus specifically as he calls him out of the grave. With Jesus being the Lord of life, just think what would have happened had he not been specific in his command. If he'd issued a more generic order, such as "Come out," the assembled onlookers would have been amazed with all of the people emerging from their graves![13]

The dead man is now alive. After all, where Jesus is, there can be no death.[14] Note in this story how much John emphasizes death and life. For instance, he calls Martha the sister of the dead man, he says the stench will flow out of the grave, and he even says, "The dead man came out" (v. 44). Perhaps he wants to highlight the gift of renewed life that Jesus gives to Lazarus.

Lazarus emerges (v. 44).[15] He's still bound with his graveclothes and, in a notable detail, has a cloth on his face. Had his limbs been bound together, he wouldn't be able to walk out of the tomb. But the Jewish people followed the Egyptian practice of wrapping each limb separately in their own bandages.[16] Yet they didn't embalm the body as the Egyptians would, removing everything from within that would decay, but would wrap the body in perfumes.[17]

As commentators from the early church have observed, Lazarus's graveclothes can symbolize the sin we find ourselves entangled in.[18] We might be bound to addictions, traumatic experiences, wrong beliefs, or a faulty self-image.[19] After we die, we'll enjoy our risen bodies and will be free from all that entangles us in sin. But for now, we can live out of the new self as through the help of the Spirit we daily shed our old selves—those graveclothes that sometimes trip us up.[20]

Jesus initiates the removal of the bandages: "Take off the grave clothes and let him go" (v. 44). Through this clear and practical command, Jesus welcomes the others to join in with this astonishing, life-giving event.[21] The church helping to remove these clothes of death is vital, says Augustine. Lazarus was "entangled with the bandages," but the believers gathered there unbind him.[22] We need each other, and Jesus, to remove the trappings of death, whether they are harmful patterns of behavior, defective beliefs, or unhealthy compulsions.

Raising Lazarus is not the first time Jesus brings someone back to life—he did so with both the son of the widow of Nain (see Luke 7:11–15) and the daughter of Jairus (8:41–42, 49–55), reviving each of them within hours of their deaths. But this is the first time he calls back to life someone who was dead four days.

Some theologians see this story as a rehearsal for Jesus's death and resurrection. For instance, Jesus weeping at the death of Lazarus is mirrored by his agony in Gethsemane (Matthew 26:36–46). The devastation of Martha and Mary parallels the anguish of the disciples and friends at his death (see John 20:11–15); and both are filled with wonder and awe when Lazarus and Jesus come back to life (Luke 24:36–44). God the Father makes all things new.

With this miracle, the religious leaders see their power slipping away. It's yet another signal to them to keep on plotting and planning. But in contrast to them, Jesus exemplifies true power.

## Loved Back to Life

I can find so much to lament over, so much pain and heartache, not only in national and international events but in the lives of those close to me. I think of a friend seeing her world constricting with a shattering health diagnosis. Another has been living in temporary housing for over a year as their house purchase fell through. Now as they renovate their new home they discover that their neighbors threaten legal action to the point that my friend cannot live in this new home. More neighbor issues for another friend as the whispering campaign against her has developed into a legal dispute. She no longer feels safe to enjoy her lovely garden. Another friend faces bullying in the workplace, the gossip and lies affecting her health.

Each of those scenarios feels like a separate tomb of sorts—the limitations of health, the injustice of gossip, the red tape of legal battles, the exhaustion that comes from being betrayed. How can I support my friends when I feel like they've entered a tomb and I stand at the sidelines? My first response is simple and heartfelt—I cry out to Jesus. When I hear the latest in the various sagas, I listen and pray, pray and listen. I give God my fears about my loved ones, my heartache, the feelings of incensed anger—all of it. Often I'll take myself on a walk when I'm overcome with someone's intense suffering, especially if I'm tempted to sort out some solutions for them. The physical act of walking while keeping an internal dialogue with God helps me to release my thoughts and feelings to him, and eventually to come to a place of if not resolution then peace.

Friendship with Jesus allows me to feel deeply with empathy and love; I have a natural boundary in expressing my angst to him because I can look to him to sort things out. Just as Martha and Mary both did when they told Jesus that Lazarus wouldn't have died had he been there.

Jesus stands outside the tombs we find ourselves trapped in and weeps. He shudders with emotion at the pain we experience. And he brings to us hope, new life, and acts of resurrection in various ways. I wish I had a list of the answered prayers to share with you about how God responded to my friends. We're too much in the messy middle for me to do so yet, but I trust and believe that God will make a way for each of them.

I believe with them, just as with Lazarus and the sisters, that Jesus doesn't give the last word to loss, grief, or anger. Nor to illness, death, or decomposition. He doesn't avoid the hard things of danger, suffering, and death, but rather offers life in the midst of them—life that sustains through trauma.[23]

Note how very grounded this miracle is—Jesus performs it at a specific place and time to particular people. He embodies light, life, love, and friendship in this sign—not in general or abstract qualities.[24] As his friends trust him, they experience his grace and love through their relationship with him.

As we see in this part of the story, this tale of two women and the brother they loved, their faith is great but not perfect. Martha dialogues with Jesus about who he is as he deepens her understanding of the truth. With Mary, he almost certainly wants to restore her belief that he loves her and that he hasn't abandoned her. Jesus as their friend takes the faith of both of them and changes it, making it new.

Jesus performs this miracle out of his love for the siblings but also bears in mind the cost it will entail—mainly the hastening of his death at the hands of the religious leaders.[25] He knows that the Jews will be incensed, and that this will be the final straw that will send him to his death. We learn that many come to faith when Jesus raises Lazarus from the dead (John 11:45). But many also turn against Jesus, including the Jews who go to the religious leaders to report what Jesus did (v. 46). After the miracle, as always, the result is division.[26] And so Jesus's road to Calvary continues in earnest. The new life of Lazarus leads to the death of Jesus.[27]

Although this story documents great joy, it also centers on lament and being honest with Jesus. Take a few moments to ponder how you're feeling about Jesus. Can you, like Martha, make a profession of faith that he is the Messiah? Or do you, like Mary, feel unseen, let down, or disappointed with the events you've experienced recently? Let's turn to prayer as we consider these questions.

## Time to Pray: At the Tomb

Our prayer exercise entails sitting by the tomb—a tomb in your imagination or one that you construct. You'll be writing out laments and burying them.

Spend some time alone with God, sharing with him an area of disappointment either in your life or in the life of someone close to you. Ask God through the Holy Spirit to bring just the right memory or person to your mind. You don't need to go digging; if nothing comes up, then pray for someone close to you. God knows you completely and loves you perfectly, so you can trust that he will bring to mind just the right matter or person for you to pray about. Consider prayerfully when you've cried out to Jesus, "Lord, if you were here . . . [something specific] wouldn't have happened."

On a piece of paper, write out your lament; document your hurt and disappointment over the situation. Release all of your feelings to God—he will receive them with grace and without judging you.

Then find a place that can act as a "tomb." Maybe you have an area of your garden where you can bury your piece of paper in the dirt. Maybe you could hide it in a bookshelf. Or slide it into the compost.

Whatever you decide to use as your tomb, go there now with your lament. As you bury the paper, give your feelings to God. Ask God to hear the cries of your heart and to release you from your hurt and disappointment. That you would not become bitter and hardened.

Then don't miss an important part of this exercise—receive from God any words of affirmation, promises, or the peace that he may have for you. Spend time enjoying his presence. What kind of gift of resurrection might Jesus have for you?

You might want to ponder the words of Charles Spurgeon: "Come forth from the grave! Come forth! Jesus calls you to come and trust him! Not only will he make you a new creature, but he promises to take you one day to where the angels dwell, above all, where he dwells. What a glorious sight that will be!"[28]

Remember that even as Jesus wept over Lazarus's death, so he weeps over our pain and sorrow. Be encouraged that we have a God who mourns with us and who makes all things new, bringing life where there was death.

❧ ❧ ❧

## The Lord Is . . .

How is Jesus the source of all life? In this rendering of Psalm 23, I focus on how he gives us life. Have you tried penning your own psalm?

> The Lord is the master of life and death, I lack nothing.
>     He gives me peace next to the tomb,
> he leads me beside living water,
>     he refreshes my aching heart and mind.
> He guides me to release my heartache and sorrow to him
>     for his honor.
> Even though I walk
>     through the deepest pain and loss,
> I will fear no evil,
>     for you are with me;
> your enveloping peace and mercy,
>     they comfort me.
> You prepare a table before me
>     in the presence of those who cannot comfort me.

You wrap me in your love;
    my peace overflows.
Surely your goodness and love will surround me
    all the days of my life,
and I will live with you and my loved ones in your house
    forever.

Questions for Individual Reflection or Group Discussion

1. How do you think you'd react if you were at your loved one's tomb and Jesus asked for the stone to be rolled away?

2. Consider and discuss the full quotation by Peter Chrysologus: "You see how he gives full scope to death. He grants free reign to the grave. He allows corruption to set in. He prohibits neither putrefaction nor stench from taking their normal course. He allows the realm of darkness to seize his friend, drag him down to the underworld, and take possession of him. He acts like this so that human hope may perish entirely and human despair reach its lowest depths. The deed he is about to accomplish may then clearly be seen to be the work of God, not of man."[29]

3. What does it mean to you that Jesus is the Lord of life?

4. Many people throughout the years have seen Lazarus's graveclothes as symbolizing the sin that can entangle us. Does this image resonate with you? Why or why not?

5. When you grieve over some kind of loss, how do you express yourself to Jesus? How does he respond? How might you do this differently in the light of this story?

## PART 3

# Loving and Serving

## The John 12 Story

In our third story, the family enjoys a banquet in Jesus's honor during the last week of his life. Martha serves, Lazarus leans on Jesus, and Mary anoints him with costly perfume. Each of the siblings shows their love for Jesus in their own unique ways. This party is a picture of the hope and the new life we have with our friend and Savior Jesus.

## CHAPTER 7

# The Party

**As I look around our dining room,** I experience a flash of unalloyed joy. Wanting to build community, I've gathered ten women to celebrate my birthday, but I haven't expected to feel so overcome with joy and gratitude as they sing "Happy Birthday" to me. As I take in their shining faces, I feel like they're giving me an unexpected gift of love.

I felt awkward in throwing myself a birthday party, but the idea had lodged within me after a friend mentioned that she hosted one with the aim of getting to know some interesting women. I loved the idea of community-building and celebrating life, but I wavered about whether to host a party. I wondered, *Will my friends think that I'm trying to grab a bunch of presents or that I want them to celebrate the great and wonderful* me?

But I decided to give it a go to build relationships among women in a similar situation—mothers with young children trying to juggle work and family. I had prayed that the evening would be a stepping stone to deeper relationships, whether at the school gate or at church. But I didn't reckon on receiving more than I give. I soak in the moment, blinking back my tears and raising my glass with a smile.

## Outpouring of Love

Jesus has loved Lazarus back to life, and his sisters want to celebrate. What could be better than a party atmosphere with good food and conversation, and Jesus the honored guest? After all, they could have been gathering to remember Lazarus with sad faces and dashed hopes. In contrast, at this joyous occasion they reverberate with laughter and thanksgiving. Instead of a funeral, Lazarus is alive!

Let's read this story of a love offering and the reaction it sparked:

Six days before the Passover, Jesus came to Bethany, where Lazarus lived, whom Jesus had raised from the dead. Here a dinner was given in Jesus' honor. Martha served, while Lazarus was among those reclining at the table with him. Then Mary took about a pint of pure nard, an expensive perfume; she poured it on Jesus' feet and wiped his feet with her hair. And the house was filled with the fragrance of the perfume.

But one of his disciples, Judas Iscariot, who was later to betray him, objected, "Why wasn't this perfume sold and the money given to the poor? It was worth a year's wages." He did not say this because he cared about the poor but because he was a thief; as keeper of the money bag, he used to help himself to what was put into it.

"Leave her alone," Jesus replied. "It was intended that she should save this perfume for the day of my burial. You will always have the poor among you, but you will not always have me."

Meanwhile a large crowd of Jews found out that Jesus was there and came, not only because of him but also to see Lazarus, whom he had raised from the dead. So the chief priests made plans to kill Lazarus as well, for on account of him many of the Jews were going over to Jesus and believing in him. (John 12:1–11)[1]

While engaging with this story of Jesus being anointed, it's helpful to note which one it is in the Gospels. Bible commentators agree that this account in John 12 is the same given by Matthew and Mark but differs from Luke's story.[2] Luke tells of a "sinful woman" in the region of Galilee who anoints the feet of Jesus a year before Jesus was crucified. While the Bethany story concerns a meal held in Simon the Leper's home, Luke's anointing happens in Simon the Pharisee's home, which tells us that he couldn't be a leper because of his prominent circumstances.[3]

John's account, however, differs slightly from those in Matthew and Mark. For instance, in John's gospel, Mary anoints Jesus's feet but in the others his head. The timing differs too, with John placing the account before Palm Sunday and the others after. One reason for John's timing may relate to Jesus as King—that John wants to emphasize Mary's anointing as anticipating Jesus's royal entry to Jerusalem.[4]

## Service with a Smile

Sometimes when we host people at the vicarage, I feel like Martha did in the Luke story—hassled and overwhelmed, the burden weighing on me as I work to make everything clean and welcoming. Other times, though, I feel moments of unadulterated joy in providing a space for rest, conversation, and fun. My gratitude for those visiting us bubbles up within me, delighting me. I wonder if this is how Martha felt in this story in John's gospel.

Our only clue about Martha, this outspoken sister we've grown to love, comes in verse 2: "Martha served." Just two words, but they entail so much. The imperfect tense in the original language implies a continuing activity—she serves throughout the meal.[5] This same verb is repeated later in the chapter when Jesus says, "Whoever serves me must follow me; and where I am, my servant also will be. My Father will honor the one who serves me" (John 12:26). In serving Jesus she honors his Father.

Martha being mentioned first in the story might imply that she plays a hosting role.[6] I like to think that her heart has changed now in her service; this is conjecture as we aren't told. Although before she complained, now she uses her gifts of hospitality in tending to Jesus. Again, she's doing the role of a man servant; she's not afraid to buck the cultural strictures in fleshing out her love for Jesus through her actions.

She hasn't become bitter or angry from Jesus's earlier challenge to follow Mary's example of sitting at his feet. And we don't see any hints of tension between her and Mary.[7] Rather Martha's grown from the earlier experience, along with that of her encounter with Jesus after her brother died.[8] She expresses extravagant love to Jesus through serving him.

I'm touched by the story of extravagant love that a friend shared with me of Brendan from County Cork in the Republic of Ireland.[9] Brendan was a recovering alcoholic who every now and then would "lose it and go off on a bender."[10] When this happened, the pub would ring the pastor, and he and some members from the church would recover Brendan, taking him home and getting him into bed.

Because of this weakness, Brendan never felt able to become a member of the church, but he wanted to repay them for their care of him. The church met in a hall on the edge of the local park and didn't have any facilities but were given keys to the public bathrooms in the park. And yes, the state of those loos was just as you might imagine! Every Saturday night Brendan put on rubber gloves and completely cleaned the toilets so that the next morning they would be fresh and nice for his church family. He poured out his extravagant love for them in a practical and hands-on way.

We too can serve extravagantly like Martha and Brendan through setting up the chairs at church, or being on the welcome team, or acting as the treasurer. Or simply through making that hot beverage for someone, or holding open the door for the person following us, or removing our headphones to help out someone in need. As I did one cold winter's day while walking home from the gym.

I was enjoying my audiobook when I came upon an older woman on her own. I noticed that she wasn't wearing gloves and asked, "Are you okay?"

As she responded, I soon realized she needed some help. She said that she'd escaped from the nasty person caring for her and that she was trying to get to her daughter's home. As I gave her my gloves, I tried to figure out where she needed to go without much success. Then I tried to call my husband to see if he could meet us with the car, but every time I tried calling, the phone would die. Eventually I decided we should just press on and try to find her daughter's home. I prayed fervently for her safety and that God would direct us.

The half hour we walked felt much longer as I fretted about Rosie and whether she was catching a chill and whether we'd make it to her daughter's home. But we kept walking, step-by-step. As we finally arrived at the interesting-looking home that I'd always wondered about, we shuffled up the stairs, with her holding my arm for support, and rang the doorbell. The man who answered the door looked questioningly at me, but then gasped as he said, "Rosie! Are you okay?"

We had found the right place, and thankfully her son-in-law was at home. As he wrapped her in a blanket and made her a cup of tea, he explained that his wife's sister took care of their mother full-time—this was no evil caretaker. And that Rosie's dementia sadly seemed to be increasing.

As I reflected later, my act of service that day didn't feel extravagant— I only gave a bit of time and an arm to lean on. But God had used me extravagantly in that family's life, keeping their beloved mother safe and from harm. To be able to help in this way made me weep with gratitude. As I extended an act of service to Rosie and her family, I grew in my friendship with God. He had helped me look outside of myself and turn off the audio-book when I could have easily kept on walking.

What acts of service could you do today? How might your love for God and others grow as you do them?

## Back for Life

If you were to place yourself in the gospel story as Lazarus, what might go through your head and heart as you feel Jesus's solid form next to you (v. 2)? Gratitude for being alive? Thankfulness for being healed? We aren't told, but if Lazarus had a chronic condition previously, he might not have been able to leave their home. Now he's at Simon's as he dines with Jesus, enjoying his company and the fellowship of others.

Indeed, Lazarus leans against the One who brought him back to life. He and the others would be stretched out on the floor and propped up on the table while eating. In terms of the action to come, Jesus's feet wouldn't be tucked underneath him.

Again we don't hear anything from Lazarus, but perhaps him simply being there is an act of love. None of us knows what happens when someone dies—and particularly those who died before the resurrection of Jesus—but if Lazarus has experienced the wonders of heaven, he may not have wanted to return to the dusty earth, a place of disease, hurt, and pain. Yet he's there with Jesus and seems at peace. That he's eating reminds those gathered of Jesus's miracle, for Lazarus is truly alive.

Consider for a moment how both Lazarus here and Mary in the Luke story were with Jesus. While Mary sat at his feet, learning from him, Lazarus reclines at the table with Jesus. Perhaps this occasion is not primarily for learning but for celebrating—he's leaning back in a mode of relaxation. Do we too take time to sit with Jesus, relaxing and just spending time with him? I know some families or groups of friends during holiday meals keep an empty chair at the table to symbolize Jesus eating with them. We too could set a place for him at our next meal and see what happens.

With Lazarus never speaking in the Bible, we can easily overlook the fact of him being a real person. My friend Bill Haley had a burst of recognition of Lazarus as the man, and what might have become of him after the gospel stories, when he visited Cyprus. While Western tradition holds that Lazarus and the sisters, in danger from the religious leaders, were put on a boat and ended up in France, Eastern tradition says that they fled to Cyprus, where Paul and Barnabas made Lazarus a bishop.[11] There in Cyprus is a second tomb of Lazarus, which my friend Bill visited. Of course we don't know the truth of either tradition, but I like to think that Lazarus led a fruitful life, passing on the wisdom he gleaned from Jesus and modeling what friendship with him looks like.

Indeed, Charles Spurgeon says that we are to envy Lazarus. Martha got to serve Jesus, but Lazarus got to commune with him. I like how Spurgeon says that we can imitate Lazarus—we too have been dead in our sins, but Jesus raises us from them, and because of his life, we now live.[12] We can imagine ourselves leaning against Jesus, soaking in his love, and receiving his affirmation as we give him our thanks and our praise.

## True Motives

Although Martha and Lazarus showed love to Jesus, giving us an example of true friendship, another character from the story reveals the opposite—Judas. His friendship with Jesus is marred and stained. Because we live in a world that isn't as God created it, affected by sin, disease, and wrongdoing, our friendships won't be perfect either. Unfortunately, we all may be able to bring to mind a story of betrayal.

I think of my friend Andrea, whom I supported from a distance when she experienced the loss of a friend through an act of duplicity. Andrea had moved to a new community, looking forward to making friends and settling in, especially as a new parent. She was delighted when Liz befriended her, and they connected on a deep level. Soon they became prayer partners, sharing their fears, joys, and challenges with each other. Andrea told me how much she appreciated Liz, especially as Liz had been a parent for longer and would happily give her tips and advice. But when their church teemed with conflict, Liz spoke about Andrea in a public meeting in a way that left Andrea reeling. She felt the betrayal deeply, wondering why she had ever trusted her in the first place—the hurt lodged within her body like a physical presence. I tried to be a listening ear for Andrea, a safe place for her to share her early disbelief over the situation, then her hurt and anger, and finally the release of her bitterness to God. Liz and Andrea never did reconcile, but God relieved Andrea from the pain of the situation.

I wonder how Jesus processed the emotions when Judas, one of his close friends, acted against him. We know he never stopped loving him, even though at this dinner, Judas sets off onto his path to the betrayal that leads to Jesus's death. Judas observes Mary's scandalous act of sacrifice and becomes enraged (vv. 4–5). From the start his words sound hollow as he protests that this perfume could have been sold and the proceeds given to the poor. The oil that Mary pours away in one lavish act, he says, is worth what a laboring man would earn in a year. One Bible version names the amount as "300 silver coins"—with Judas later accepting a tenth of that when he betrays Jesus.[13]

Consider how vocally Judas objects to Mary's love gift—perhaps he's actually attacking Jesus by stealth for accepting this gift. Mary could appear an easier and more vulnerable target to release his anger on than Jesus. How do we similarly displace our ill feelings against God on those near us, such as family members or friends? This can be an uncomfortable insight, especially if we, however subtly, target someone who might inhabit a weaker position than we hold.

Note how Judas tries to cheapen Mary's generous gift by stating its monetary worth.[14] But John names Judas's true motives. As the group's treasurer, Judas has an eye on the money for his own purposes. He's motivated not by love for those in need but because he wants a cut of what would have been a very large amount of cash. A greedy person always needs more.

I appreciate how popular writer Liz Curtis Higgs draws a contrast between Judas and Mary: Judas is greedy and Mary generous; Judas betrays Jesus while Mary remains loyal; Judas hasn't got a clue how to worship Jesus while Mary not only knows how but does.[15] The two seem to be polar opposites; one a true friend, the other not.

I might be quick to judge Judas, but I know that I too can be motivated by stuff. A memory comes to mind of some years ago when I noticed an older woman from our church at the grocery store. Delighted to see her, I put my items of food behind hers ready to be checked out. We chatted about our families, and then as she was leaving, with a smile she handed me a twenty-pound note to pay for my items.

Afterward I felt a niggle in my conscience. Did I go talk to her eagerly because deep down I thought I might benefit from the encounter? (This wasn't her first act of generosity—she came from a culture of honoring the pastor and his wife.) I had to admit that my motives were mixed.

In his account of this story, Mark reports that not only Judas objects to Mary's anointing, but that Jesus's disciples also berate her "harshly" (14:5). Even Jesus's closest friends can't see the point of this extravagant gift as they join in the groupthink to criticize her. She's not the first nor the last woman to receive such censoring.

## The Defender

His friends might offer a not-so-helpful critique of Mary, but not Jesus. He, loving Mary and understanding her motivations, defends her, telling them to leave her alone and saying what a beautiful thing she's done for him (Mark 14:6). As a true friend, Jesus stands up for her in her devotion, just as he did when Martha wanted Mary to join her in the kitchen. Mary is the only woman in the Gospels that he defends twice in this way.

Jesus knows that she's preparing for his burial (14:8); he notes how she's saved the perfume for this moment (John 12:7). In the original language, the word for *saved* means "to guard or to hold fast." Interestingly, it's the same word that appears in Jesus's first miracle at Cana—that the best wine was saved for last (see John 2).[16]

Jesus then names Judas's greed, noting that the poor will always be there to help, but that he won't be. He guards and protects her act of love. Mark adds Jesus's comment that the disciples can help the poor at any time.

Jesus in his defense of Mary utters a short line that jumps out at me: "She did what she could" (Mark 14:8).[17] Because I often think I can accomplish more than I can, at least without reaching a breaking point, I ponder these words of Jesus. Mary's act is simple—pouring oil on the feet of Jesus. But her unbounded love has rocked the world for thousands of years. She acts out of her limitations and does what she can to show her love for her friend.

I too can acknowledge the challenges I face, whether physical, financial, or emotional, but then out of my relationship with Jesus, I do what I can. For instance, a friend from up north has asked if she can stay at the vicarage a month from now. I'd love to say yes but know I need to say no as we'll be moving out of the vicarage the following week for needed renovations. I can, however, invite her over for a meal. I'll do what I can.

Let's recap the role of the characters who play the supporting position in this story before we move to Mary in the next chapter. Martha served, pouring out her love on Jesus in this practical manner. Lazarus lived, leaning on Jesus and enjoying his company. Judas turned on Jesus, expressing his anger and selfish motives through his critique of Mary's beautiful gift of love.

How do we, like Martha, serve Jesus? How do we, like Lazarus, lean on him? How do we, like Judas, turn on our Friend? And a bonus question about Judas—how can we continue to love those who betray us (acknowledging that this might entail the need for boundaries)? You could take some time writing out your thoughts and reflections in each of these areas, or going on a walk to ponder them, or chatting about them with a friend.

## Time to Pray: Cupping and Releasing

When we're the subject of gossip or when someone close to us betrays us, our pain can morph into bitterness. We might or might not feel called to forgive the perpetrator—for instance, if they remain unrepentant we might want to leave any forgiveness to God. But we can look to God for comfort and peace through prayer.

Let's pray:

*Lord, quiet my heart as I come to you. I thank you that you are with me and that you love me sacrificially. You sent your only Son to suffer betrayal and a whispering campaign the likes I've never experienced. Then Jesus died on the cross, taking my place. You now welcome me to come to your table. Through your Spirit, I ask you to reveal to me now what only you can. Guide and lead me into life; release me from something that keeps me from embracing and giving love.*

Cup your hands as if you're holding a butterfly.

*Lord, as I hold my hands cupped together, show me anything I might have cupped in my heart and mind and body that I'm keeping from you. What am I squirreling away, perhaps in fear? Show me any anxieties or perhaps a nudge from you that I've been ignoring—that friend or family member I can't yet forgive or that step of faith I fear taking.*

Your hands might feel sore from cupping them together as we pause before God. You might long for release but not know how to relinquish the fears, the whatever, your cupped hands symbolize. Continue to pause before God.

Now hold your cupped hands out from your body as you prepare to give those things to God.

*Lord, the act of giving and releasing can be difficult. Please give me the faith to release to you whatever is in my hands. I hold them cupped but away from my body as an act of faith. Please help me next to move to the step of release.*

Open your hands and release what's inside, and then stay with your palms facing upward to receive from God.

*Father God, as I release to you whatever was in my hands; I ask that you take those things or people and to redeem them. Turn them into*

*something beautiful—or even more beautiful—for your sake. Help me
as I hold my palms out to you, to receive your healing and release and
empowering. I want to step into any commission you might be giving
me, whether an act of sacrifice, an act of love, or something new to
create. Empower me to love and live and learn for your name's sake.*

Spend some time receiving from God whatever he may want to give to you.
Don't strive; simply rest in his presence. After a few moments, you might
want to write down any thoughts or insights you have received.

❦ ❦ ❦

The Lord Is . . .

We've seen how Jesus defends Mary against detractors. He will be our
defender too. Adapting Psalm 23 along these lines feels powerful:

> The Lord is my defender, I lack nothing.
>> He takes me away from the circles of gossip,
> he leads me to spaces of peace and rest,
>> he restores me after I've been attacked.
> He guides me along the right paths
>> for the praise of his name.
> Even though I walk
>> through devastating betrayals,
> I will fear no whispering campaigns,
>> for you are with me;
> your knowledge of the truth,
>> it comforts me.
> You prepare a table before me
>> in the presence of those who speak against me.
> You cleanse me with living water;
>> I'm free and clean.
> Surely your goodness and love will accompany me
>> all the days of my life,
> and I will dwell in your house
>> forever.

Questions for Individual Reflection or Group Discussion

1.  Consider Martha in this story. What do you think has changed for her as we've traveled with her in these three stories? What's the same?

2.  Now think about Lazarus. How has your view of him changed throughout these stories? Why?

3.  Today I glimpsed a post on social media that relayed that the test of the Christian faith is not loving Jesus; it's loving Judas. Do you agree or disagree? Why?

4.  Jesus said of Mary, "She did what she could" (Mark 14:8). How could you apply this maxim to your life? Would it change anything about how you live?

5.  How do we see Jesus expressing his friendship to each of the three siblings in this story? How might he be showing his love for and his friendship with you?

# CHAPTER 8

# Liquid Love

**On Valentine's Day,** I sit at the front of the chapel at Ridley Hall, Cambridge, holding hands with my husband. Although we've been married less than a month, we're renewing our vows—it's our English celebration following our wedding in Virginia. Sitting next to me is Kathy, with whom I exchange a smile. I'm so glad she's traveled over to be my best woman, shlepping along a suitcase of my possessions.

I think about all of the people filling the chapel, most of whom I'm meeting for the first or second time. They are Nicholas's family and friends, and I wonder which ones will become my close friends. Only Kathy has flown over for the service, but two other Americans are also present, Mike and Susanne, who work at Ridley Hall and have lived in the United Kingdom for years. As Mike gives the sermon, I turn back my attention to focus on what he's saying.

He speaks powerfully about the passage we asked him to address, the story in John 12 of Mary anointing Jesus with precious nard. Nicholas and I see this text as symbolizing the liquid love that we want to receive and exude through our life together with God. Mary's example of extravagant love is one we want to emulate, although at this early stage neither of us understands what that will entail.

## Anointing the Anointed One

I've just returned to my desk after hanging out a load of laundry outside, the bright summer sunshine promising to dry the clothes quickly. As I came back inside I broke off a sprig of lavender and inhaled deeply. Sniffing the lavender as I write—even through my miserable cold—reminds me of the gifts God gives us in creation. And if lowly but lovely lavender can encourage me so much, what would a pint of pure nard spark in me?

That's what we see Mary pouring out on Jesus. Let's revisit this portion of the story:

> Six days before the Passover, Jesus came to Bethany, where Lazarus lived, whom Jesus had raised from the dead. Here a dinner was given in Jesus' honor. Martha served, while Lazarus was among those reclining at the table with him. Then Mary took about a pint of pure nard, an expensive perfume; she poured it on Jesus' feet and wiped his feet with her hair. And the house was filled with the fragrance of the perfume. (John 12:1–3)

This aromatic oil was made from the roots and stems of a flowering plant grown in the Himalayas and had a very thick consistency. This perfume smelled like gladiolas and had a red color. It was used in a variety of ways, such as in recipes for medicine, as an aromatic wine, a breath scent, and a perfume for clothes and the body.[1] It was also used as a spice at a funeral to mask the stench of death and decay. In the Old Testament, nard was the main ingredient of the perfume to make the consecrated incense, the Ketoret. The priests would offer this incense on the altar of the temple.[2]

In breaking off the seal at the top of the container, Mary snaps off its neck. There'd be no going back after doing so; the scent would waft out immediately. Eventually the aroma would be smelled up to half a mile away, so intense is this scent.[3]

Mary holds nothing back as she bathes Jesus's feet, soaking the edge of his hem with this precious ointment (v. 3). Could we follow Mary in a similar act of utter humility and devotion? When I imagine imitating Mary, I can feel myself flushing with shame as I'd anticipate what people would say about me with such an extravagant act. Even as Jesus's friends criticized Mary, as we explored.

She anoints his feet and not his head, as was the usual practice for festive occasions.[4] In ancient Israel, kings, priests, and sometimes prophets would be anointed from above, their head bathed in oil. But Mary anoints his feet from below as an act of humility. She takes on the task of the lowest slave in attending to Jesus's feet.[5]

In anointing Jesus Mary acknowledges his true status as King. Her anointing doesn't bestow the title of King to him as he already inhabits that title, but she makes known his true identity on Earth.[6] The name for Jesus, *Messiah* or *Christ*, affirms this truth as it means "anointed one." The next day Jesus will acknowledge that title as he enters Jerusalem triumphantly, the people waving their palm branches while shouting: "Blessed is the king of Israel!" (v. 13).

Mary focuses only on Jesus as she disregards even more social conventions when in a scandalous act she wipes his feet with her hair (v. 3). Only wives or sex workers would do something so intimate, and certainly not in public. But Mary lowers her hair in an act of devotion seemingly as pure as the precious ointment she pours out on Jesus.

Sometimes I'm stingy in my giving. I hold back a bit or more of my heart; I don't give everything with abandon. I think that if I retain just a little for me, I won't lose myself. But when, convicted by the Spirit, I examine my motives and actions before God, I ask myself, How can I too pour out the expensive perfume of my life?

When I think about Mary's gift, given from her place of deep security through her friendship with Jesus, the pure nard seems almost like a sacrament—an outward sign of an inner reality. Her pouring out of liquid love is an act of devotion and sacrifice.

## Opening Our Hearts

After speaking about the siblings at Bethany a couple of years ago, I received a lovely email from one of the day's participants. She said how she'd been considering what it means to give extravagantly. Although she doesn't usually compare herself to others, she found that lately she felt like her prayer life and relationship with Jesus was wanting. Mainly because she'd been praying for her sisters and brothers living in persecution because of their faith, and she wondered if she too would be faithful to God in those stark circumstances.

While prayerfully pondering how she could continue to pour out her love extravagantly on Jesus, she came to a clear understanding that she didn't need to compare herself with others. That Jesus received her prayers for these dear ones suffering for their faith as an act of extravagant love. She felt set free from the niggles that had been troubling her as she understood that she needed to be faithful to the task she felt God calling her to—that of the work of prayer.

The extravagant giving of Mary entails different things to different people. For instance, to one person it might mean opening their heart just a crack but to another it might mean flinging the door open. And God doesn't force us to open our hearts wide. But as we even creak open the door a tiny bit, he sends his slivers of light and love to flood through within, shining on us and transforming our world.

We're all different, and we might prefer for our major focus in giving to be financial. I have friends who give away a large portion of their income to causes close to their hearts. Instead of buying flashy cars or spending time in lavish hotels in far-flung places, they choose to give their money to help those in need and to promote the good news of Jesus. I have other friends whose income might be less than others, but they also give sacrificially.

How about you? What's your current level of giving, either financially, through volunteer work, or through opening your heart to others? Might you consider doing a giving audit? You could prayerfully look at the various aspects of your life to see how you might increase what you give away.

## An Unpredictable Reach

In pouring out the oil on Jesus, Mary too becomes anointed with this fragrance. In the original language, the word for *nard* is *pisitke* (pure), and it has shades of meaning including believing, having faith, and trusting.[7] All of which Mary exudes in her act, which unites her to Jesus through the shared scent, touch, and her acceptance of his death.[8] What a contrast this "scent event" is to the decomposing of Lazarus.[9]

With Mary's anointing, the house fills with the fragrance of the perfume as her private act becomes public, the scent spreading not only throughout Simon's home but beyond. Mary pours out on Jesus her most prized possession, what would have been her personal dowry, saved to present to the groom's family as a gift.[10] When Jesus hung on the cross, this royal scent probably remained. In the anguish of those moments, perhaps he had a whiff of her love, her abundant gift.

What wafts out from the broken jar evokes the mystery and beauty of the Holy Spirit. Like the air that carries the fragrance, the Spirit crosses boundaries and spreads unpredictably.[11] This echoes what Jesus said of those born of the Spirit: "The wind blows wherever it pleases. You hear its sound, but you cannot tell where it comes from or where it is going" (John 3:8).

Mary is a woman of insight who prepares for the death of Jesus. Indeed, she's the first person to anticipate his death, and she doesn't try to stop or hinder it.[12] Instead she anoints his body in the pure nard that the priests use at the temple, as I mentioned earlier, evoking the scent of worship there. This hearkens back to Jesus earlier telling his friends that his crucified and resurrected body would be the new temple (see John 2:19–21).[13] Her insights into what will happen have been birthed in her relationship with Jesus. She's in tune with him, listening for and noticing the things that others may have missed.

In Mary's anointing we witness the fruit of her friendship with Jesus. She who sat at his feet, learning from him, pondered his teaching and soaked in his love. She who expressed her desperation over Lazarus dying, crying at his feet, received his comfort. Now she pours out her deep gratitude in a loving act so profound and lasting that even we these thousands of years later continue to ponder it.

When I think of Mary's great gift, I remember the faithful and quiet witness of our friend Margaret. Although she faced physical limitations, eventually becoming housebound, she was an active member of our church before she died as she dedicated herself in the work of God in the church and around the world. My husband would often call her up and, while respecting confidentiality, would share with her some of the challenges he experienced as the church minister. She'd listen and then pray through the concerns. Just how God answered those prayers I'll never know, but I'm guessing that God's Spirit moved powerfully in response. Her sacrificial gift transformed her patch of North London.

At times I feel like my extravagant gift, my pouring out of liquid love, is to embrace life in the UK year after year. When I married Nicholas, he was in his final year of training to become a minister in the Church of England, and our thought was that we'd stay here for five to seven years and then move to the States with its wide highways and stellar plumbing. With some twenty-five years in the UK, I have seen those plans come to naught!

At times living here has felt less sacrificial than others: Being in London for the Olympic Games in 2012 with the wonderful spirit of camaraderie and welcome. Raising kids without the fears of school shootings. Exploring the amazing countryside and the accompanying history and culture. Reaching the point of embrace by Brits that they grace me with their irony and banter, even if it still flies over my head. And so many more wonderful aspects of life on this small island.

But I miss high-school graduations and weddings, Christmases and Easters, gatherings of friends and sitting by hospital beds. Knowing we won't be together, we purchase birthday and Christmas gifts ahead of time to avoid costly postage fees. The Atlantic felt particularly impassable during the pandemic, as month after month the travel restrictions kept me from loved ones.

Yet I've gained so much in living here, even if at times I feel like my giving is extravagant and I'm pouring out my life in one big heap of precious oil—something I could be tempted to hold back and hoard. Through these years I've learned that in losing ourselves, we find ourselves; in losing what we hold dear, we can yet unearth treasures that would otherwise remain buried. For me, in leaving my country with my friends, family, and work behind, I've yet found my identity in Christ deepened. I love being a wife and mother within these shores. And I've discovered different roles that might not have been available to me in the States as I moved from editor to writer and speaker, retreat leader, and spiritual director. I continue to ask God to help me pour out my precious oil as a gift of love for him.

## The God of Abundance

God is the source and the definition of liquid love:

> Liquid love—
>     the pure nard poured out in devotion
>     the stuff of my creation
>     my sweat in Gethsemane
>     my blood that I shed for my children
>     the cup that you drink in communion with me
>     my cleansing, living water
>     my healing oil
>     what I, the giver of all good things, give you

God's love poured out on us transforms us, changing us from stingy to generous. From controlling and manipulative to loving and warm. From worrying and anxious to trusting and hoping.

His liquid love changes us, repairing our broken relationships. He gives us love for those whom we thought we couldn't love or forgive, such as in-laws or betrayers or family members or friends.

His liquid love brings hope. We can see past our hard circumstances; the anguish and loss. We can believe that God will redeem the pain, that he will bring healing and hope and grace—even if that healing might be fulfilled on the other side of the grave.

His liquid love brings joy, belonging, meaning, and peace. It radiates the sweet fragrance that fills the home so that all who enter will smell, feel, and experience it.

The liquid love of pure nard is what God's people can give back to him. We can pour it out without fear. We don't need to be sparing in its release, for we can trust that there will be enough.

For our God is an extravagant God. He holds nothing back—not even his only Son. And he will not hold back the floodgates of his love. God is the source of our giving; he's a God of abundance, not scarcity. He lavishes all of his resources on us.

His liquid love is freely available. He pours himself out for us that we may pour out his love to others. And he bids us, *come. Come to the waters, all*

*who are thirsty, come and eat and drink. Why spend money on what does not sat-
isfy? Come and eat and drink and be filled. Come to the waters* (Isaiah 55:1–2).
Amen. May it be so.

## Time to Pray: Receive God's Promises

In their sermons, two of the early church writers, Athanasius and Augustine, spoke out the words of God to their listeners so that they could inter-
nalize them. In this prayer exercise, we'll engage with these words from
God to those whom he loves, chewing on them as we ask God to help us
believe them.

Receive the words as God's gift to you, and engage with them. You
might wish to read through or hear them more than once. As you do so, you
could write or draw your response:

> Come forth. See, I am standing by you. I am your Lord (Isaiah 41:10).[14]
> You are the work of my hands (64:8).[15] Why have you not known me,
> because in the beginning I myself formed Adam from the earth and
> gave him breath? (Genesis 2:7).[16] Open your mouth yourself so that I
> may give you breath.[17]

> Behold, the prophecy of Isaiah the prophet will be fulfilled in you,
> namely, "I shall open your tombs, and I shall bring you forth" (Isaiah
> 25:8).[18] After all, I am not the God of the dead but of the living (Mark
> 12:27).[19] I am the voice of life that wakens the dead.[20] For if you believe
> in me, though you were dead you will live. If you do not believe in me,
> even while you are alive you are dead (John 11:25).[21]

> I am the good odor that takes away the foul odor of sin and death.[22] I
> command the foul odor to depart from you. For I am the sweet odor of
> eternal life, where you will live among the trees of paradise.[23]

> Stand on your feet and receive strength for yourself. For I am the
> strength of the whole creation. Stretch out your hands, and I shall give
> them strength (Isaiah 41:10).[24] For I am the straight staff (Psalm 23:4).[25]

I am the voice of joy that takes away sorrow and grief (Jeremiah 33:10–11).[26] I comfort those who grieve (Psalm 34:18).[27] And I give joy to those who belong to me. I gladden all my friends and rejoice with them. I am the joy of the whole world (Romans 15:13).[28]

I call my own by name (Isaiah 43:1).[29]
I am the bread of life (John 6:48).[30]
I am the gate by which Lazarus reenters the world of the living (10:7).[31]
I am the good shepherd who protects my flock from the world (10:11).[32]
I am the resurrection and the life (11:25).[33]
I give you all of this at the price of my own life.[34]
I am the way, the truth, and the life (14:6).[35]
I am the true vine (15:1).[36]

I love you (Isaiah 43:4).[37]
You are my beloved (1 John 3:1).[38]
You are mine (Isaiah 43:1).[39]
When you seek me with all your heart you will find me (Jeremiah 29:13).[40]
I will never leave you nor forsake you (Deuteronomy 31:8).[41]
I love you (John 15:9).[42]

❧  ❧  ❧

The Lord Is . . .

Jesus is Mary's beloved friend and companion. Can we too express a deep devotion to Jesus, so much so that we'd pour out a year's worth of precious possessions on him? Let's follow Psalm 23 in this theme:

> The Lord is my friend, I lack nothing.
>     He makes me lie down in places of safety,
>  he leads me to refreshing, quiet waters,
>     he cares for my spiritual, emotional, and physical health.

He guides me along the right ways
    for the honor of his name.
Even though I walk
    through times of pain and loneliness,
I will fear no abandonment,
    for you are with me;
your compass and your walking stick,
    they guide and help me.
You prepare a table before me
    among those who distract me.
You walk right next to me;
    my joy and contentment overflow.
Surely your love and encouragement will follow me
    all the days of my life,
and I will enjoy your love and your friendship
    forever.

## Questions for Individual Reflection or Group Discussion

1. How do you react to Mary's extravagant gift—her using the nard that would have equaled a whole year's wages? Consider and discuss what such a gift would look like in your life.

2. Mary's anointing of Jesus is an acknowledgment of his status already as King. Why do you think this matters?

3. What does extravagant giving look like to you?

4. Mary in anointing Jesus also becomes covered in this costly perfume. How do we receive when we're the ones giving?

5. As far as we know, Mary was the first to anticipate the death of Jesus. Why do you think that is?

# The Encounter That Changes Us

We reach the end of this journey with Jesus and the beloved siblings from Bethany, but our life with God continues. As we consider their friendship and our own, why not call to mind any of the friends you thought of when reading the book's introduction? I hope you've held them in your heart as you've read—those who grant you welcome in their soul, just as you welcome them into yours. How has your understanding of friendship changed over the course of engaging with these three stories from the Gospels? How are you becoming a better friend? As you consider these questions, ponder if there's something you could do to cultivate and deepen those particular relationships.

I think about the special ones I've held close as I've met with Jesus and the siblings. I smile at the image of a friend who exudes a deep generosity of spirit as she gives of herself. Of the former colleague who after our first meeting welcomed me as a kindred spirit. Of those in my life who may exude a hard exterior but who foster a loving heart underneath. Truly, friendship is a most precious gift.

And our best friendship is with God, he who loves us and gently changes us to be more like Jesus. We've seen how he affirmed Mary in her sitting at his feet while acknowledging Martha's desire to serve and yet calling her to a better way. Similarly, in our friendship with God, we grow and flourish as we learn from Jesus and serve him with joy.

We've seen how Jesus met both Martha and Mary in their grief, dialoguing with Martha and expanding her faith in him while joining Mary in her sorrow. We've witnessed him resurrecting Lazarus, moving him from death to life. When times are hard, our friendship with God upholds us. We have a safe space to share all of our pain and anguish with him, and he meets us right where we're at. He brings us hope and new life, changing our despair into joy.

And we've seen how all of the siblings showed Jesus their love at the celebratory dinner: Martha through serving, Lazarus through leaning on Jesus, and Mary through anointing him with precious oil. We can celebrate and rejoice with Jesus, the giver of life.

I think of Carol's journey of accepting her husband's upcoming death by cancer. She and her husband, who was known as Papa John because of the fatherly love he exuded, discerned from God that he would receive his final healing through death. They came to this understanding through prayer and wise counsel, and felt that in sharing their journey they could embody how to trust God in *all* circumstances. And so they did. Witnessing their love for each other and for Jesus gave me hope and strengthened my faith. Their anticipation of, and acceptance of, Papa John's death grew out of their strong relationship with God.[1]

Life has its ups and downs—from the anguish of Lazarus's death to the unbridled joy of his resurrection and all of the times in between and after. Our friendship with Jesus undergirds our life just as it did for Mary, Martha, and Lazarus. Just as the sisters turned to Jesus for help, so too we can ask God to intervene in our lives, whether we're wrestling over a wayward child or crying out to God to stop injustice or waiting for him to answer our heartfelt pleas. He hears us and will answer according to his mercy and grace.

As we walk day by day with Jesus, sharing our joys and our sorrows, he will meet with us. He'll never leave us to wallow alone but will take our hand in his, giving us peace even as we grieve or rejoice. He'll inspire us to serve him with our gifts and talents, and he'll welcome us to lean on him. What a Friend! What a Savior!

May our lives reverberate with the glories of friendship with God.

# Acknowledgments

Writing is not only a solitary but a community affair, and I'm so grateful for the amazing group of people who have brought this book-baby into being. You embody the friendship I write about—thank you!

To my publishers on both sides of the Atlantic, thank you for supporting me in this venture, for your passion and vision for spreading God's love among your readers. I feel so thankful to call you my publishers. To my friends at Our Daily Bread Publishing in Grand Rapids: Thank you, Dawn and Chriscynethia, for your leadership and care. Dawn, I love how you helped harvest the kernel of friendship from the early material. Anna, you've been a fabulous editor, helping me to see what needed unraveling and to state things more clearly. Thank you too to the marketing, publicity, and sales teams who make the process a smooth one, with a special shout-out to Melissa, Kat, and Cathy. To my friends at SPCK/Form: Elizabeth, you are a wonderful powerhouse, and I love working with you! Your creativity, get-things-done spirit, and generous approach fill me with joy. Thank you to Sam, Wendy, Rowan, Rhoda, and now I get to work with Lawrie and Dave again too? Dream team.

Thank you to my prayer people—Ali, Anne, and Julie, who pray me through the days and the nights, and the intercessors who faithfully support me and my family. I'll say it again, in the apt words of Lord Tennyson: "More things are wrought by prayer than this world dreams of." I could say so much more, but please know that my gratitude runs deep and wide.

To Tanya and Amy, my weekly and sometimes daily writing partners, I'm so grateful for how God has intertwined our lives. Tanya, your fingerprints are all over this book as you pushed and prodded and helped me to apply and dig and explore. Just wow—thank you.

Thank you to Nicholas, J, and A for living through another book. Nicholas, you're my primary cheerleader and you enable me to spend my days this way—thank you. To our lovely kids, I pray as you reach new stages in your life that you'll continue to flourish and grow, that you'll enjoy a deep and rich friendship with Jesus, and that you'll have many lifelong friends to love and be loved by.

And to my friends, the true treasure in life. My cup overflows! I'd love to spend pages and pages listing each one of you individually but will picture you instead and breathe a prayer of gratitude for the ways you enrich my life. May you know God's love and grace as you share your unique gifts with your families and communities.

# Leader's Guide

Thank you for choosing *Transforming Love* for your small group! I trust as you engage with these gospel stories that the relationships within your group will deepen as well. God loves to strengthen our friendship with him and others.

## Before You Start

As you prepare for your meetings, make praying before each session a priority, trusting that God will guide you as you lead. Spend time lifting each person in your group before God, one by one, noting anything that comes to mind. You might be surprised at what creative ideas emerge that you might not have otherwise considered. God will be an active partner in your meetings!

Leading can be tricky if one or more people tend to fill every available opening with their comments. You can affirm their contributions while gently drawing out the quieter members of your group. You might have to resort to speaking to the more vociferous members on their own at the end of the session, asking them to help you encourage others to engage fully during the meetings.

My advice for leading the prayer exercises is to leave enough time and silence for God to work. We might be tempted to rush ahead as we might feel awkward and wonder what's going on with everyone during these moments of silence. I often set the stopwatch on my phone to make sure I give everyone enough time for each prayer practice. As I lead more and more prayer exercises, my confidence grows and I'm more able to embrace the silence as I remember the amazing ways people share that God meets them.

During the times of prayer, the members of your group may wish to write out their thoughts and prayers in a journal, either on paper or on their device. Remind them also to bring along their Bibles (which of course they might access on their phone).

I recommend leaving enough space for people to share how they met God during the prayer exercise, if that feels safe for them to do so. It's good to cultivate a time of sharing with a spirit of thanksgiving and not critique. I find hearing from people in this way hugely encouraging and wonderful.

## A Sample Timeline

You may have your own tried-and-true pattern for your meetings, but here's a suggestion for how to run an hour-and-a-half meeting.

### Welcome and Opening Prayer (Up to 5 Minutes)

Open your meeting with prayer, welcoming God as an active participant and your close friend. You might want to pray something like this:

> *Loving God, thank you for bringing us together. We welcome you to guide us and encourage us as we engage with these wonderful gospel stories. Spark hope in our hearts as we learn more about Jesus, and help us to find out more about ourselves too. Keep us away from all that is evil and help us to exercise discernment and grace with each other. We welcome you and look forward to how you will work in our lives. In the mighty name of Jesus we pray, amen.*

### Warm-Up Activity (10 Minutes)

If your group is newly formed, you might want to start off with an opening activity to set the scene. You could begin with something as simple as introductions, including an open-ended question such as "Share a favorite childhood memory" or "My favorite food is . . ." Or you might want to come up with an activity based on the theme of the meeting.

## Introducing the Topic (15 to 20 Minutes)

Using the chapter as your guide, give a short introduction to the gospel story you will look at together and the focus of the particular meeting. You might want to start with having someone read aloud the story from Luke's or John's gospel. Give some of the background and history, and don't be afraid to share what you think of the various characters and their actions, and how Jesus responds to them.

## Questions for Discussion (15 to 20 Minutes)

At the end of each chapter, I've included five questions that you can use as launching points for your group's discussion. As you move through the questions, gently exercise your leadership as needed, returning people to the topic at hand if the discussion moves off of it.

## Prayer Practice (20 to 25 Minutes)

Time to pray! Lead the group through the prayer practice, and note the particular guidance I give for each of the chapters in what follows here. I hope you will find this part of your meeting a fruitful, wonderful time of communion with God. I suggest making the prayer activities the focal point of your meeting, as you pray that each person will encounter God.

You may also wish to set aside some time for people to write out their version of Psalm 23, based on the theme of the chapter. Sharing these aloud will be mutually encouraging.

## Closing Prayer (5 Minutes)

Close your meeting in prayer, thanking God for being with you as you commit yourselves to following him during the coming week. Here's an example:

> *Father, Son, and Holy Spirit, we thank you that we can come together in your presence. Thank you for Jesus and for the stories of how he interacted with these beloved siblings from Bethany. Solidify in our hearts and minds what we've been learning together, that we might continue to deepen our friendship with you. Guard us and guide us when we are apart. We pray in the name of Jesus, amen.*

# Notes on the Prayer Exercises

## 1. So Distracted—Prayerful Reading

Simply read out the instructions as you lead this exercise, trusting that God will work in the lives of those in your group. Don't be afraid to give enough time of silence after each of the four steps (I'd recommend around three minutes for each step). Some leaders prefer to play some instrumental music during the pauses, but I usually only do so when I'm giving seven or more minutes of silence. You might feel awkward, wondering if the moments without words are far too long and if God is doing anything. That's natural! Just set a timer on your phone and trust that God is meeting with his people.

At the end of the exercise, leave enough space for those in your small group to share how God met them (as much as they feel comfortable with). Your sense of encouragement will grow with each story as you hear the wonderful ways God reveals himself.

## 2. Listening and Learning—Sitting at the Feet of Jesus

As you lead the prayer practice, follow the instructions in the chapter. Start with a prayer asking God to help you all encounter him as you go through the story. Read through the passage aloud once or twice to the group so that they are familiar with it. Then lead them through the story, adding details and questions that will help them enter into the scene. They may wish to engage by closing their eyes or by writing down the thoughts that come to them.

For instance, what do they see, hear, smell, feel? Who are they in the story? What are they doing? Allow enough time for silence so they can enter into the action. Bring the exercise to a close with a prayer of thanks and dedication, and then allow time for people to share about their experience.

## 3. Both . . . And—Looking Back to Move Forward

To engage with this prayer exercise, introduce this way of praying that looks back to move ahead. This type of prayer can be especially helpful in discerning how we are with God. Read the introductory paragraphs, and if it doesn't feel too vulnerable for your situation, pose the two questions for group discussion or for discussion in pairs (What makes you forget or ignore Jesus? Where have you overcommitted yourself?).

Make sure you pray at the start of the prayer practice, asking God to lead and guide and to keep his people's hearts open and discerning. Then give your group paper and pens, or ask them to write on their phones, as they engage with the five steps of the prayer. One way is to lead them through each step, giving them three minutes to focus on it before you introduce the next step. Or you can give them a set amount of time to engage on their own, such as fifteen minutes.

After you call the group back, pray with thanks for what God has been doing and ask him to continue this work in them through his Holy Spirit. Ask also that anything not of him would drop away. Then host a time of sharing how they encountered God and what they learned and discerned.

## 4. Waiting for Jesus—Praying with the Psalms

As we join Mary and Martha in a stance of waiting, we use the prayer book of the Bible—the Psalms—to help us voice our feelings to God. Here I recommend praying through Psalm 27. In the chapter I give an example of how to pray through it, which you can read out over the group, leaving space for them to interact with it, or you can send them off for a set amount of time to do so on their own. You will know your people, and will discern whether it's best to read out the prayers in a group or for them to engage individually. A benefit of doing it together is that it's a shared experience and you'll ensure that they work through the whole psalm. A challenge of doing it together is that you might have to move them along to the next section before they are ready. Whichever way you choose, reassure them that God will meet with them, and that they can always pick up any loose ends later.

If you choose to read out the psalm bit by bit, I suggest following the pattern I give in the chapter of dividing it into eight segments. It's up to you whether or not you include my examples of how I interacted with it. I suggest giving up to two minutes to pause for each section of the psalm.

## 5. Aftermath—Learning to Lament

Again we engage with one of the psalms as we lament, this time Psalm 22. We follow David's fourfold pattern of expressing himself to God through *address, complaint, request,* and *expression of trust.*

Begin by introducing the prayer practice, sharing what everyone will do, and read through Psalm 22. Next, read my example based on the story of Mary and Martha. Then allow people to engage on their own for a set amount of time—perhaps ten minutes. When they return, ask them to share their laments, if they feel comfortable in doing so.

## 6. At the Tomb—At the Tomb

For this prayer exercise you'll need some slips of paper and writing utensils, and you will either construct something or find some place that will act as a tomb. If you want to make a tomb, you could use a cardboard box, laid on its side with the top open and flaps cut off. Using another piece of cardboard, cut a large circle that will act as the stone that covers the opening of the tomb. Or as I say in the chapter, you could find a space in your garden to bury the piece of paper—if it's feasible to take everyone outside. Or slide it into the compost. Or hide the paper in a bookshelf (but tell them not to hide it so well that you cannot retrieve it easily later!). Assure them that no one will read what is on the paper, so that they can be totally open and honest with God.

Share the purpose of the prayer exercise with your group and give the instructions for how they will interact with the tomb. Then lead them through the prayer practice, allowing them time to engage with God and to bring to mind which person or memory they want to pray through. When they are ready, they can bury the paper as a symbol of giving it to God. Encourage them to wait on God after releasing this to him, as he may have words of love, encouragement, or wisdom to give to them. It can be easy to miss this important part of the exercise, but it can be a precious time of connecting with God.

At the end of the exercise, depending on what you chose for your tomb, retrieve the bits of paper and destroy them without reading them. Or there are other creative approaches too. For example, once when I led this exercise on a retreat, I retrieved the paper from the stack of logs we used as a tomb. We had a bonfire that night, and I gave each person one of the slips of paper—and instructed them not to read it as it probably wasn't their own! Everyone took some time to prayerfully place the paper on the fire. We found it a moving and enriching experience.

## 7. The Party—Cupping and Releasing

This prayer exercise is best done with you reading the instructions and prayers I include in the exercise out over your group, so that they can receive from God and engage with him. Encourage them to quiet themselves and close their eyes, if that feels most comfortable. At the end of the exercise, give them some time to write out what they experienced and then to share with others if they wish to do so.

## 8. Liquid Love—Receive God's Promises

As this is a shorter prayer exercise, you could read over the words of the prayer twice to let them sink in more deeply, giving people time in between to engage with God's promises. Again allow some space at the end for group members to finish jotting down any notes and insights.

As this is the last session on this topic, spend some time sharing how you all have grown in friendship with God over the weeks. Discuss too how people discern the friendships within the group have changed and deepened. If you've not had time to read out any of the renditions of Psalm 23, take some time to do so now.

You could end your meeting with a celebratory meal, or with dessert, to add some time of festive fellowship.

# Notes

## Introduction: Friends of Jesus

1. Ben Witherington III, *Women in the Ministry of Jesus: A Study of Jesus' Attitudes to Women and Their Roles as Reflected in His Earthly Life* (Cambridge, UK: Cambridge University Press, 1984), 100.

2. William A. Barry, SJ, *A Friendship Like No Other: Experiencing God's Amazing Embrace* (Chicago: Loyola Press, 2008), xiv.

3. See https://amyboucherpye.com/books/transforming-love/.

## Chapter 1: So Distracted

1. Witherington, *Women in the Ministry of Jesus*, 100.

2. Their financial situation isn't outlined in the gospel stories, but we can assume the family had some wealth, not least because Mary was able to purchase the expensive perfume, as we'll see in the John 12 story. Clarence L. Haynes Jr., "6 Things to Know about Mary and Martha in the Bible," Bible Study Tools, April 25, 2022, https://www.biblestudytools.com/bible-study/topical-studies/things-to-know-about-mary-and-martha-in-the-bible.html.

3. Bruce J. Malina and Richard L. Rohrbaugh, *Social-Science Commentary on the Synoptic Gospels* (Minneapolis: Fortress Press, 1992), 348, quoted in Sophia Austin, "Choosing the Part of Discipleship: Re-focusing Our Interpretations of Luke 10:38–42" (unpublished paper, Anabaptist Mennonite Biblical Seminary, 2018), 3.

4. For a discussion of Lazarus's illness, see, for instance, William Lynes, "Lazarus, Forensic Pathology of the Bible," LynesOnline.com, last modified March 22, 2021, https://www.lynesonline.com/post/lazarus-forensic-pathology-of-the-bible.

5. Miriam Feinberg Vamosh, *Women at the Time of the Bible* (Herzlia, Israel: Palphot, 2007), 20, in Liz Curtis Higgs, *The Women of Easter: Encounter the Savior with Mary of Bethany, Mary of Nazareth, and Mary Magdalene* (Colorado Springs: WaterBrook, 2018), loc. 245 of 3811, Kindle.

6. Witherington, *Women in the Ministry of Jesus*, 101.

7. Allie M. Ernst, *Martha from the Margins: The Authority of Martha in Early Christian Tradition* (Boston: Brill, 2009), 197.

8. Ernst, *Martha from the Margins*, 199.

9. In conversation I've adopted the question my husband employs: "How do you spend your time?"

10. I'm so grateful to Jonathan Burnside for this practice. My website has lots of examples (The Lord is my . . . Producer; Surgeon; Reviewer; and so on), https://amyboucherpye.com/category/christian-life/psalm-23/.

## Chapter 2: Listening and Learning

1. Evelyn and Frank Stagg, *Woman in the World of Jesus* (Edinburgh: Saint Andrew Press, 1978), 118.

2. Carolyn Custis James, *When Life and Beliefs Collide: How Knowing God Makes a Difference* (Grand Rapids, MI: Zondervan, 2001), 35–36.

3. "Mary is commended for *choosing*, not for being passive." Richard Bolling Vinson, *Luke: Smith & Helwys Bible Commentary* (Macon, GA: Smyth & Helwys Publishing, 2008), 11, quoted and emphasized in Austin, "Choosing the Part of Discipleship," 10.

4. As observed by Augustine: "But the Lord replied on Mary's behalf, and, although he was called upon as her judge, himself became her advocate." Augustine, Dom Morin, and E. J. B. Fry, "Martha and Mary: The Two Lives," *The Life of the Spirit* 2, no. 22 (December 1945): 170.

5. See Augustine, Sermons 179 and 255, in *The Works of Saint Augustine: A Translation for the 21st Century; Sermons*, trans. Edmund Hill, OP, ed. John E. Rotelle, OSA (New York: New City Press, 1992), 5:148–229.

6. Augustine, Morin, and Fry, "Martha and Mary," 174.

7. I love the wink Augustine gives here: "I'm lingering on the point, because I'm enjoying it too." Augustine, Sermon 179, 5:301.

8. Augustine, 5:301.

9. Gregory the Great was born around AD 540 and died in AD 604.

10. Giles Constable, *Three Studies in Medieval Religious and Social Thought: The Interpretation of Mary and Martha, the Ideal of the Imitation of Christ, the Orders of Society* (Cambridge, UK: Cambridge University Press, 1995), 20.

11. Constable, *Three Studies*, 12.

12. Thomas à Kempis was born in AD 1379 or 1380 and died in AD 1471, and Spanish mystic John of the Cross lived from AD 1542 to 1591; Constable, *Three Studies*, 13.

13. Origen was born about AD 185 and died about AD 253; Constable, 16.

## Chapter 3: Both . . . And

1. What's a spiritual director? The term is inherited and feels a bit dated; a better phrase today would be a "spiritual accompanier." Someone who notices with a person where God is moving in their life and how they respond to him.

2. As we saw in the previous chapter, many of the early writers, such as John Cassian, Bernard of Clairvaux, Augustine, Thomas à Kempis, and later Martin Luther, were captured by the story of Mary and Martha from Luke's gospel.

3. Virginia Stem Owens, *Daughters of Eve: Women of the Bible Speak to Women of Today* (Colorado Springs: NavPress, 1995), 146, in Higgs, *Women of Easter*, loc. 191 of 3811, Kindle.

4. Augustine, Morin, and Fry, "Martha and Mary," 170. Also: ". . . that in these two women the two lives are figured, the life present, and the life to come, the life of labour, and the life of quiet, the life of sorrow, and the life of blessedness, the life temporal, and the life eternal." Sermon 54.4; quoted in Ernst, *Martha from the Margins*, 217.

5. Augustine, Morin, and Fry, "Martha and Mary," 170.

6. Constable, *Three Studies*, 19.

7. Ernst, *Martha from the Margins*, 215.

8. Saint Aelred of Rievaulx, "Martha and Mary," *The Life of the Spirit* 8, no. 89 (November 1953): 215.

9. Saint Aelred, "Martha and Mary," 216.

10. Constable, *Three Studies*, 126.

11. Message exchange between the author and Ali Grafham, April 3, 2022. Used by permission.

12. The visitor came to see Abba Sylvanus, who lived in Sinai and Syria in the late fourth century.

13. Benedicta Ward, *The Sayings of the Desert Fathers: The Alphabetical Collection* (London: Mowbray, 1975), quoted in Ernst, *Martha from the Margins*, 220.

14. See the story of how Samuel learned to discern—after several times of God calling him—how to hear God in 1 Samuel 3.

## Chapter 4: Waiting for Jesus

1. In 1998 I was still a couple of years away from having a mobile phone—my first was a brick phone. I'm not sure why I didn't have a laptop computer when first married; my only connection to the States was my big bulky Macintosh.

2. Witherington, *Women in the Ministry of Jesus*, 107. Ernst, *Martha from the Margins*, 26: "The faith of many coming to believe because of him is not linked to any action or word of him—rather of Jesus' action of raising him from the dead. Lazarus appears more like an object than a character in the narrative."

3. C. K. Barrett, *The Gospel According to St. John: An Introduction with Commentary and Notes on the Greek Text* (London: SPCK, 1956), 322; Frederic Louis Godet, *Commentary on John's Gospel* (Grand Rapids, MI: Kregel, 1978), 729.

4. The seven signs are

1. Changing water into wine (John 2:1–11)
2. Healing the royal official's son (4:46–54)
3. Healing the paralyzed man by the pool (5:1–18)
4. Feeding the five thousand with loaves and fish (6:1–14)
5. Walking on the water (6:15–25)
6. Healing a man born blind (9:1–41)
7. Raising Lazarus from the dead (11:1–44)

And the seven "I am" statements are

1. "I am the bread of life" (6:35)
2. "I am the light of the world" (8:12)
3. "I am the gate" (10:9)
4. "I am the good shepherd" (10:11)
5. "I am the resurrection and the life" (11:25)
6. "I am the way and the truth and the life" (14:6)
7. "I am the true vine" (15:1)

5. Francis Moloney, "The Faith of Martha and Mary: A Narrative Approach to John 11:17–40," *Biblica* 75, no. 4 (1994): 484.

6. John Fenton, *Finding the Way through John* (London: Bloomsbury, 1995), 70.

7. I love this about the signs from the very readable new commentary by David F. Ford: "They began with a wedding; they end with a funeral." David F. Ford, *The Gospel of John: A Theological Commentary* (Grand Rapids, MI: Baker Academic, 2021), 215.

8. Godet puts it well, that the raising of Lazarus isn't the cause of Jesus's death but hastens it. "The cup was full; this made it overflow." Godet, *Commentary on John's Gospel*, 751.

9. As Ford says, he "not only weeps but says he's the resurrection and life." Ford, *Gospel of John*, 215.

10. Dolores Kimball, *Memorial: The Mystery of Mary of Bethany* (Darlington, UK: Evangelical Press, 2014), 56–57.

11. We aren't told how much before Jesus's ride into Jerusalem on a donkey Lazarus's death was.

12. Godet, *Commentary on John's Gospel*, 732.

13. Frederick Dale Bruner, *The Gospel of John: A Commentary* (Grand Rapids, MI: Eerdmans, 2012), 660, quoted in Higgs, *Women of Easter*, loc. 332 of 3811, Kindle.

14. Higgs, *Women of Easter*, loc. 333 of 3811, Kindle.

15. "The love between Jesus and Lazarus, Martha, and Mary is repeatedly stressed—this is the first time Jesus is said to love any particular people." Ford, *Gospel of John*, 215.

16. Godet, *Commentary on John's Gospel*, 731.

17. Augustine, "Tractates on the Gospel of John 49.5," in *Ancient Christian Commentary on Scripture: New Testament*, ed. Joel C. Elowsky and Thomas C. Oden (Downers Grove, IL: InterVarsity Press, 2007), 4B:2.

18. Leon Morris, *The Gospel According to John: The English Text with Introduction, Exposition and Notes* (London: Marshall, Morgan & Scott, 1971), 540.

19. Michael J. Wilkins, David E. Garland, Darrell L. Bock, Gary M. Burge, and Ajith Fernando, *NIV Application Commentary Bundle 6: Gospels, Acts* (Grand Rapids, MI: Zondervan, 2015), loc. 65800 of 92807, Kindle. But Barrett thinks that this four-day wait was probably "far-fetched," and that it's more likely that John wants the reader to know that Jesus isn't propelled into action by anyone. Barrett, *Gospel According to St. John*, 325.

20. Not mostly dead, like Westley in *The Princess Bride*.

21. Joseph Parker, "July 5 (devotion)," in *Day by Day through the Gospel of John: 365 Timeless Devotions from Classic Writers*, ed. Lance Wubbels (Minneapolis: Bethany House, 2018), July 5.

22. Parker, *Day by Day*, July 5.

23. Morris, *Gospel According to John*, 542.

24. Morris, 543.

25. A common observation that biblical commentators make. Godet, *Commentary on John's Gospel*, 734; Morris, *Gospel According to John*, 540.

26. Ford, *Gospel of John*, 218.

27. Matthew Henry, "John 11:7," *Matthew Henry's Concise Commentary*, Bible Hub, accessed November 16, 2022, https://biblehub.com/commentaries/john/11-7.htm.

28. Parker, *Day by Day*, July 5.

## Chapter 5: Aftermath

1. Morris, *Gospel According to John*, 547.

2. Kimball, *Memorial*, 65.

3. Robert L. Thomas, *New American Standard Exhaustive Concordance of the Bible: Hebrew–Aramaic and Greek Dictionaries: Th–Alef/A–Ω* (Nashville: Holman, 1981), para 1672 + muthos 1667, quoted in Higgs, *Women of Easter*, loc. 435 of 3811, Kindle.

4. Moloney, *Faith of Martha and Mary*, 474.

5. Higgs, *Women of Easter*, loc. 428 of 3811, Kindle.

6. Augustine, "Tractates," 4B:13.

7. Moloney, *Faith of Martha and Mary*, 474.

8. Ford, *Gospel of John*, 216.

9. Godet, *Commentary on John's Gospel*, 742.

10. Higgs, *Women of Easter*, loc. 519 of 3811, Kindle; Kimball, *Memorial*, 95.

11. Theodore of Mopsuestia, "Commentary on John 5.11.29," in *Ancient Christian Commentary on Scripture*, 18.

12. Witherington, *Women in the Ministry of Jesus*, 109.

13. Morris, *Gospel According to John*, 555.

14. Witherington, *Women in the Ministry of Jesus*, 109.

15. A common theme in the commentaries; see, for instance, *NIVAC*, loc. 65861 of 92807, Kindle; Morris, *Gospel According to John*, 556; Ford, *Gospel of John*, 222.

16. Moloney, *Faith of Martha and Mary*, 487.

17. Morris, *Gospel According to John*, 558.

18. Charles Spurgeon, *Day by Day*, July 11.

19. Godet, *Commentary on John's Gospel*, 743.

20. Ford, *Gospel of John*, 222.

21. Being "signed off of work" might be unclear outside of the UK. It's when a doctor makes an official declaration that the person needs time off of work to recover.

22. I share this way of praying through Psalm 22 in *7 Ways to Pray: Time-Tested Practices for Encountering God* (Colorado Springs: NavPress and London: SPCK, 2021), 94–97.

23. Elena Bosetti, *Meditating with Scripture: John's Gospel* (Abingdon, UK: BRF, 2010), 76.

24. Parker, *Day by Day*, July 8.

## Chapter 6: At the Tomb

1. Moloney, *Faith of Martha and Mary*, 484.

2. Timothy Keller, *Encounters with Jesus: Unexpected Answers to Life's Biggest Questions* (London: Hodder, 2013), 53.

3. Hippolytus, "On the Gospel of John and the Resurrection of Lazarus," in *Ancient Christian Commentary on Scripture*, 24.

4. The full comment is lovely: "In the tomb is the stench of death. In the house—and at the burial of Jesus—is the perfume of life." Ernst, *Martha from the Margins*, 40.

5. Godet, *Commentary on John's Gospel*, 747.

6. For a fascinating look at Lazarus's death from a physician's point of view—a clinical pathology report—see Lynes, "Lazarus, Forensic Pathology of the Bible."

7. Witherington, *Women in the Ministry of Jesus*, 108.

8. We have seven of his prayers recorded in the Gospels, with this one the first in John's gospel.

9. Andrea Skevington, *Jesus said, "I Am": Finding Life in the Everyday* (Abingdon, UK: BRF, 2019), 95.

10. Peter Chrysologus was born about AD 380 and died about AD 450; Peter Chrysologus, Sermon 63.2, in *Ancient Christian Commentary on Scripture*, 4B:2.

11. As John Calvin observed: "Whatever may be [God's] delay, he never sleeps, and never forgets his people." John Calvin, *Commentary on John's Gospel*, 1:350, Christian Classics Ethereal Library, accessed March 5, 2020, https://www.ccel.org/ccel/calvin/calcom34.

12. As Ford observes, "This is the authority of a love that is willing to die." Ford, *Gospel of John*, 226.

13. I first heard of this fascinating notion from Micha Jazz when we were taping some sessions of the online course for *The Prayers of Jesus*. He told me that Clive Calver had alerted him to it. I was delighted then to find this reference from many more years before Micha and Clive: "For all the dead would have arisen out of their graves on hearing that one voice if he'd not called out one single name. Therefore he spoke in the particular." Maximinus, Sermon 14.3, in *Ancient Christian Commentary on Scripture*, 29.

14. Parker, *Day by Day*, July 8.

15. Augustine says he's "quickened by a hidden grace within." Bruner, *Gospel of John*, 685, quoted in Higgs, *Women of Easter*, loc. 674 of 3811, Kindle.

16. Godet, *Commentary on John's Gospel*, 750.

17. Godet, 747.

18. See, for instance, Irenaeus, "Against Heresies 5.13.1," in *Ancient Christian Commentary on Scripture*, 31.

19. Ford, *Gospel of John*, 226.

20. See Paul's letter to the Ephesians (4:22–24) about embracing the new self while putting off the old. The verbs in these verses are active and continuous, meaning we need to keep putting on our new selves daily.

21. Ford, *Gospel of John*, 226.

22. Augustine, Sermon 67.3, in *Ancient Christian Commentary on Scripture*, 4B:31.

23. Ford, *Gospel of John*, 281.

24. Ford, 219.

25. Godet, *Commentary on John's Gospel*, 750.

26. Morris, *Gospel According to John*, 562.

27. L. William Countryman, *The Mystical Way in the Fourth Gospel: Crossing Over into God* (Valley Forge, PA: Trinity Press, 1994), 85.

28. Spurgeon, *Day by Day*, July 14.

29. Chrysologus, Sermon 63.2, 4B:2.

## Chapter 7: The Party

1. This chapter in John's gospel provides a transition from Jesus's public ministry, including the seven miracles, to his private time with his friends before his execution and rising from the dead. David Cook, *Journey through John: 50 Daily Insights from God's Word* (Grand Rapids, MI: Our Daily Bread Publishing, 2018), 58. And while Martha features more prominently in chapter 11, Mary does more in chapter 12. Ford, *Gospel of John*, 232.

2. Matthew 26:6–13; Mark 14:3–9; and Luke 7:36–50.

3. Although Simon the Leper has this name, he'd have been healed from the disease or they'd be breaking the Mosaic law in meeting at his home—they would become unclean. He's healed and clean but the label has stuck. Higgs, *Women of Easter*, loc. 809 of 3811, Kindle.

4. On the differences between the stories, I've drawn from Higgs, *Women of Easter*, loc. 848 of 3811, Kindle; Morris, *Gospel According to John*, 572–74; and Barrett, *Gospel According to St. John*, 341.

5. Morris, *Gospel According to John*, 575.

6. Morris, 575.

7. "Death can have such a unifying effect, allowing the essentials to be seen more clearly, in particular the importance of key relationships." Ford, *Gospel of John*, 232.

8. Bill Crowder, *One Thing Is Necessary: The Wisdom of a Christ-Centered Life* (Grand Rapids, MI: Our Daily Bread Publishing, 2022), 82.

9. It's been so many years and I can't remember which friend shared this story on social media with me, but it still moves me.

10. As shared by the friend of Brendan. For those not familiar with this term, "bender" is slang for a continued use of drugs or alcohol.

11. See, for instance, "Saint Lazarus Church and the Tomb of the Man Jesus Raised from the Dead," Ancient Origins, last modified December 25, 2018,

https://www.ancient-origins.net/ancient-places-europe/saint-lazarus-church
-0011219.

12. Spurgeon, *Day by Day*, July 18.

13. Contemporary English Version. Copyright © 1991, 1992, 1995 by American Bible Society. Used by permission.

14. Higgs, *Women of Easter*, loc. 949 of 3811, Kindle.

15. Higgs, loc. 969 of 3811, Kindle.

16. Kimball, *Memorial*, 73.

17. See Elisa Morgan's *She Did What She Could: Five Words of Jesus That Will Change Your Life* (Carol Stream, IL: Tyndale House, 2017).

## Chapter 8: Liquid Love

1. *NIVAC*, loc. 66305 of 92807, Kindle.

2. Ford, *Gospel of John*, 233.

3. Lindsay Hardin Freeman, *Bible Women: All Their Words and Why They Matter* (Cincinnati: Forward Movement, 2014), 428, in Higgs, *Women of Easter*, loc. 934 of 3811, Kindle.

4. Morris, *Gospel According to John*, 579.

5. Morris, 576.

6. Countryman, *Mystical Way*, 87–88.

7. Ford, *Gospel of John*, 234.

8. Ford, 235.

9. Ford, 233.

10. See Song of Songs 1:12. K. T. Sim, insight to "She Did What She Could," by Elisa Morgan, *Our Daily Bread*, May 19, 2021; https://odb.org/GB/2021/05/19/she-did-what-she-could-2.

11. I love Ford's fuller quotation: "Like the air that carries it, fragrance also evokes the Spirit: encompassing and edgeless; spreading unpredictably and crossing boundaries; connecting with potent memories and deep relationships." Ford, *Gospel of John*, 233.

12. Moloney, *Faith of Martha and Mary*, 493.

13. Ford, *Gospel of John*, 233.

14. Isaiah 41:10: "So do not fear, for I am with you; do not be dismayed, for I am your God."

15. Isaiah 64:8: "Yet you, LORD, are our Father. We are the clay, you are the potter; we are all the work of your hand."

16. Genesis 2:7: "Then the LORD God formed a man from the dust of the ground and breathed into his nostrils the breath of life, and the man became a living being."

17. Athanasius, "Homily on the Resurrection of Lazarus," in *Ancient Christian Commentary on Scripture*, 4B:30.

18. Isaiah 25:8: "He will swallow up death forever." Athanasius, "Homily," 4B:30.

19. Mark 12:27: "He is not the God of the dead, but of the living." Augustine, "Tractates," 4B:15.

20. Athanasius, "Homily," 4B:13.

21. John 11:25: "Jesus said to her, 'I am the resurrection and the life. The one who believes in me will live, even though they die.'" Augustine, "Tractates," 4B:15.

22. Athanasius, "Homily," 4B:13.

23. Athanasius, 4B:30.

24. Isaiah 41:10: "I will strengthen you and help you."

25. Psalm 23:4: "Your rod and your staff, they comfort me." Athanasius, 4B:30.

26. Jeremiah 33:10–11: "'Yet in the towns of Judah and the streets of Jerusalem that are deserted, inhabited by neither people nor animals, there will be heard once more the sounds of joy and gladness, the voices of bride and bridegroom, and the voices of those who bring thank offerings to the house of the LORD, saying, "Give thanks to the LORD Almighty, for the LORD is good; his love endures forever." For I will restore the fortunes of the land as they were before,' says the LORD." Athanasius, 4B:13.

27. Psalm 34:18: "The LORD is close to the brokenhearted and saves those who are crushed in spirit." Athanasius, 4B:13.

28. Romans 15:13: "May the God of hope fill you with all joy and peace as you trust in him." Athanasius, 4B:13.

29. Isaiah 43:1: "I have summoned you by name; you are mine."

30. John 6:48: "I am the bread of life." Athanasius, 4B:13.

31. John 10:7: "Therefore Jesus said again, 'Very truly I tell you, I am the gate for the sheep.'" Countryman, *Mystical Way*, 84.

32. John 10:11: "I am the good shepherd. The good shepherd lays down his life for the sheep." Countryman, *Mystical Way*, 84.

33. John 11:25: "I am the resurrection and the life. The one who believes in me will live, even though they die."

34. Countryman, *Mystical Way*, 84.

35. John 14:6: "Jesus answered, 'I am the way and the truth and the life. No one comes to the Father except through me.'"

36. John 15:1: "I am the true vine, and my Father is the gardener."

37. Isaiah 43:4: "Since you are precious and honored in my sight, and because I love you, I will give people in exchange for you, nations in exchange for your life."

38. 1 John 3:1: "See what great love the Father has lavished on us, that we should be called children of God!"

39. Isaiah 43:1: "Do not fear, for I have redeemed you; I have summoned you by name; you are mine."

40. Jeremiah 29:13: "You will seek me and find me when you seek me with all your heart."

41. Deuteronomy 31:8: "The LORD himself goes before you and will be with you; he will never leave you nor forsake you."

42. John 15:9: "As the Father has loved me, so have I loved you. Now remain in my love."

## Final Words: The Encounter That Changes Us

1. I wrote about Papa John and Carol in "Trusting God in Times of Sorrow," *Our Daily Bread*, July 28, 2020, https://odb.org/US/2020/07/28/trusting-god-in -times-of-sorrow.

# Spread the Word
# by Doing One Thing.

- Give a copy of this book as a gift.

- Share the QR code link via your social media.

- Write a review of this book on your blog, favorite
  bookseller's website, or at ODB.org/store.

- Recommend this book to your church, small
  group, or book club.

**Connect with us.** 🅕 📷 🐦

Our Daily Bread Publishing
PO Box 3566, Grand Rapids, MI 49501, USA
Email: books@odb.org